Regina Liebler
Bullet Journal Inspiration

AF221179

Regina Liebler

Bullet Journal Inspiration

über 1200
Schmuckelemente

Vorlagen für
Tracker & Co.

farbig gestaltete
Inspirationsseiten

Bibliografische Information der Deutschen Nationalbibliothek:
Die Deutsche Nationalbibliothek verzeichnet diese Publikation in der
Deutschen Nationalbibliografie; detaillierte bibliografische Daten sind im
Internet über http://dnb.dnb.de abrufbar.

© 2021 Regina Liebler

Herstellung und Verlag: BoD – Books on Demand, Norderstedt

ISBN: 978-3-7534-4406-2

Inhaltsverzeichnis

Dividers

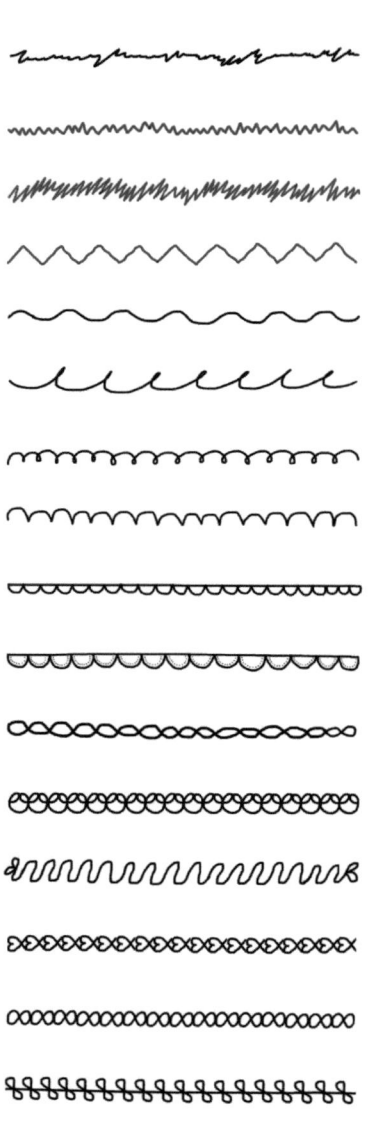
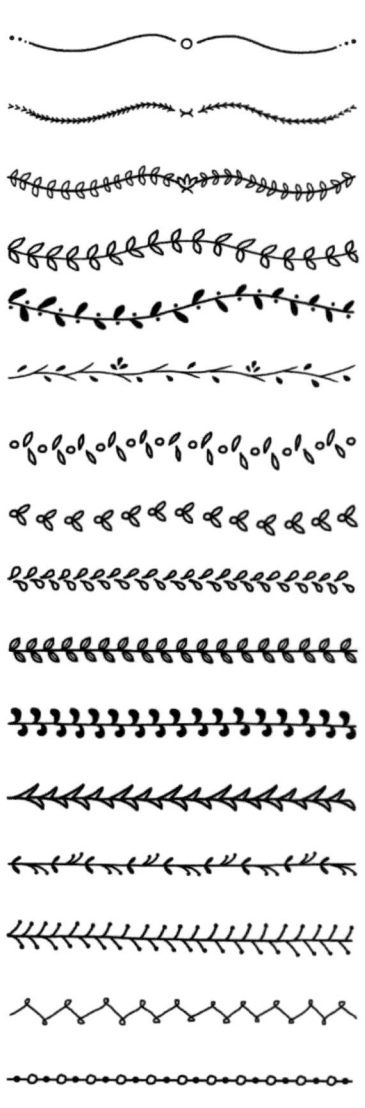

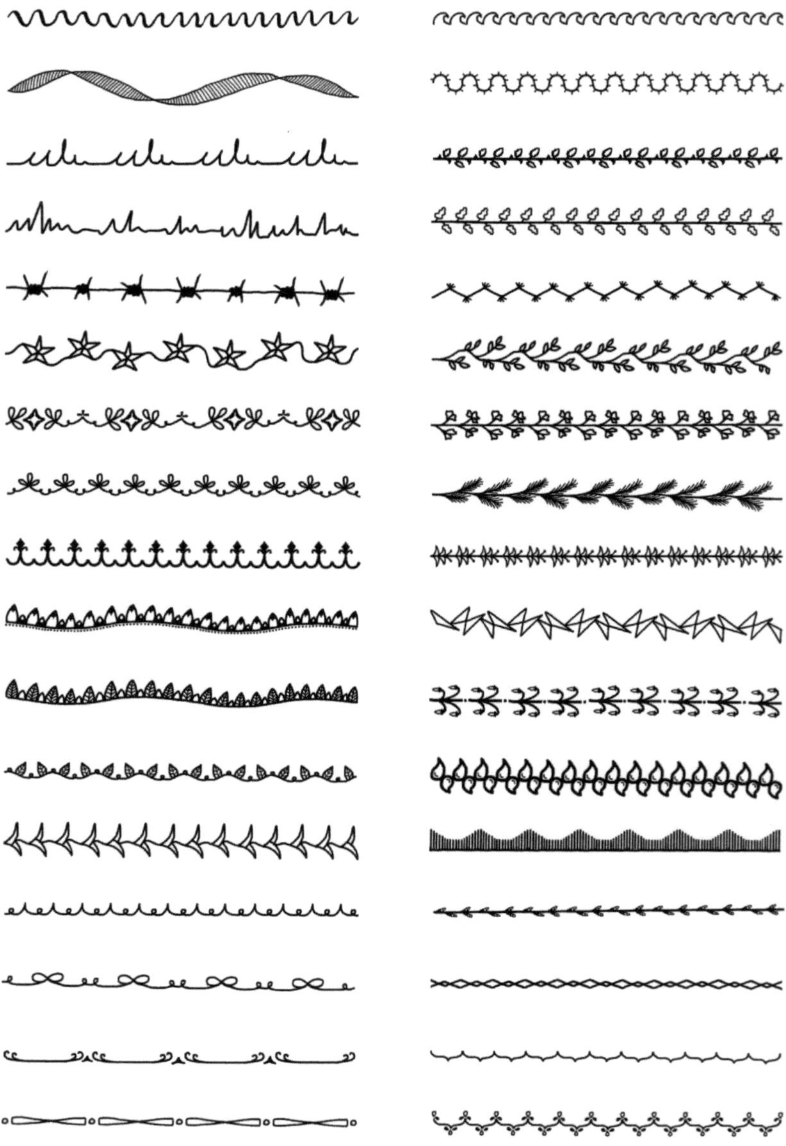

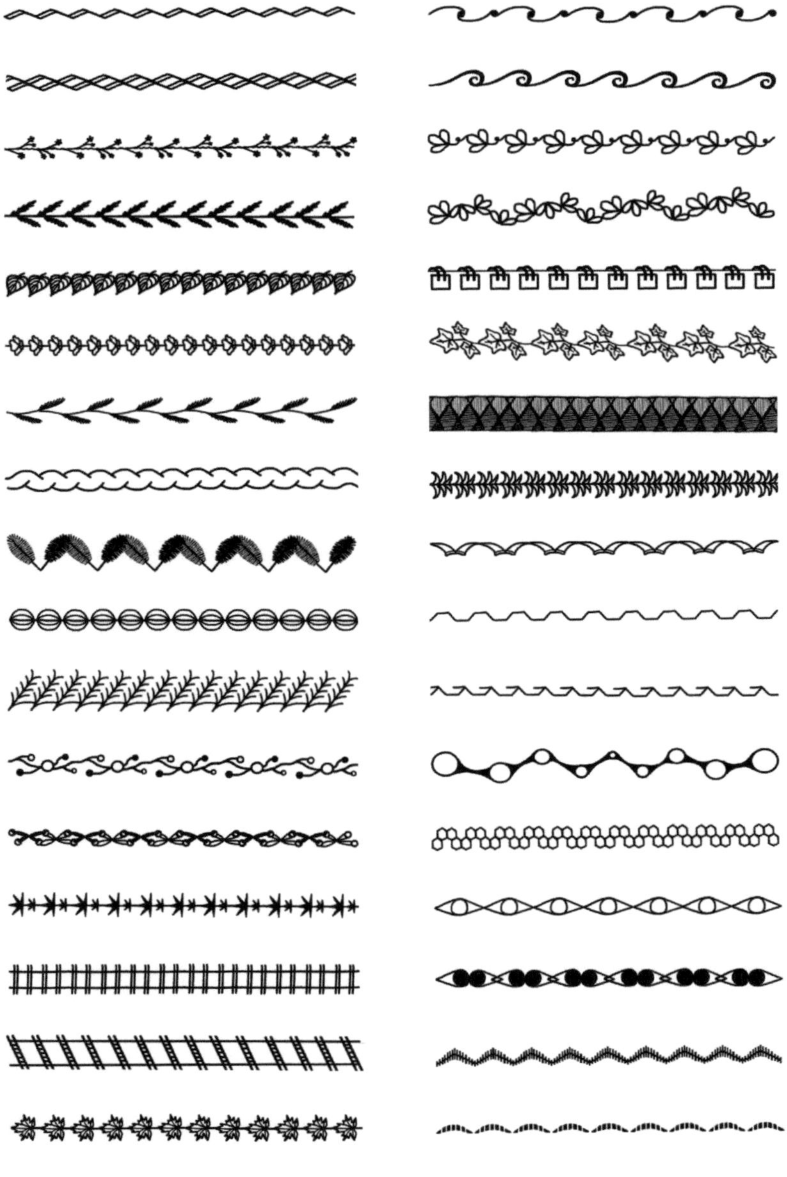

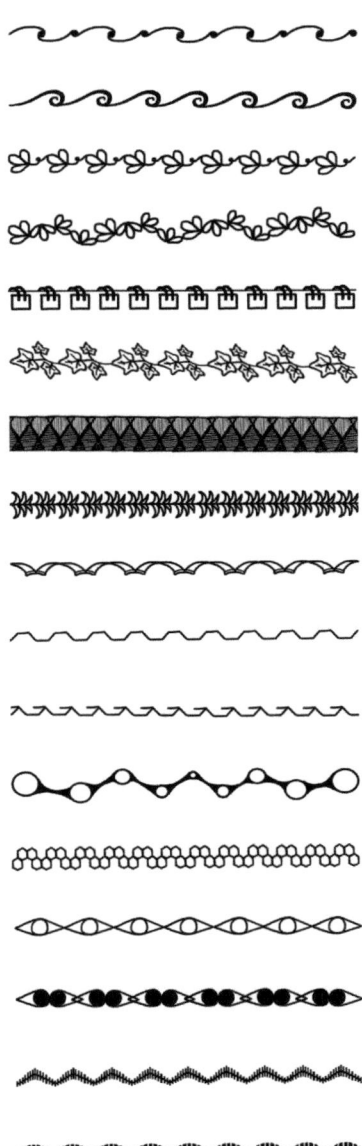

13

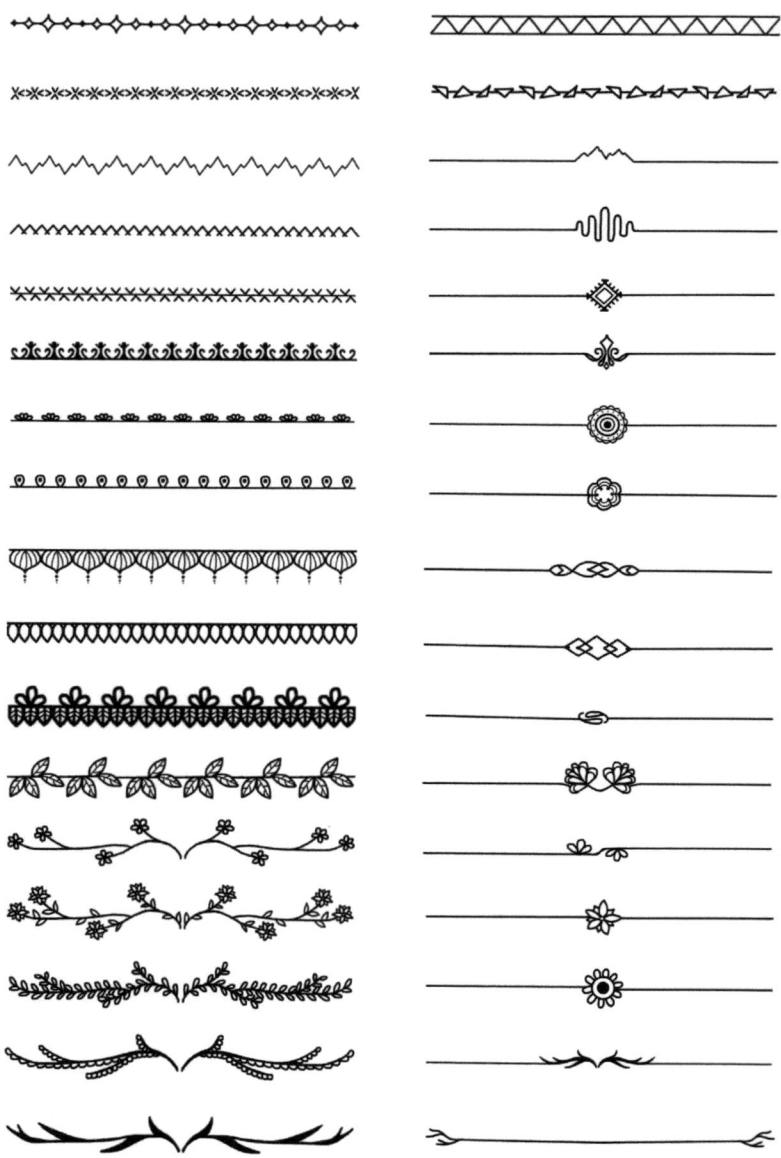

14

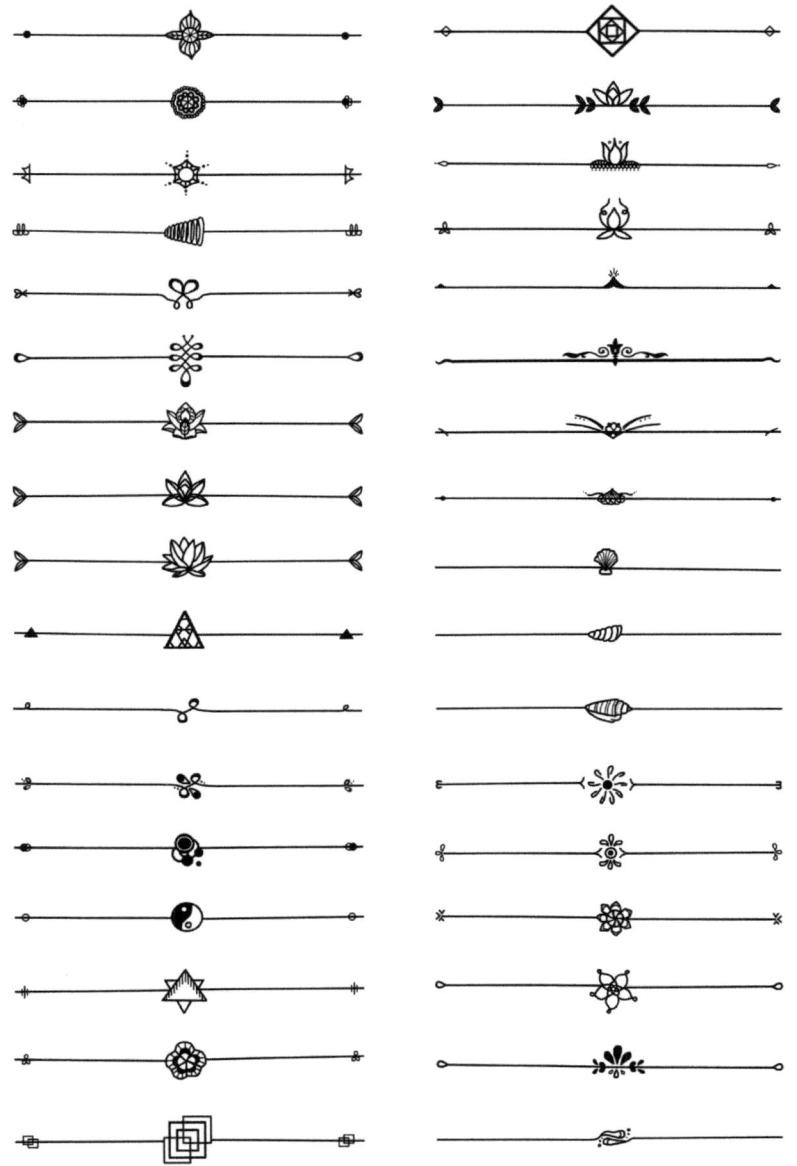

15

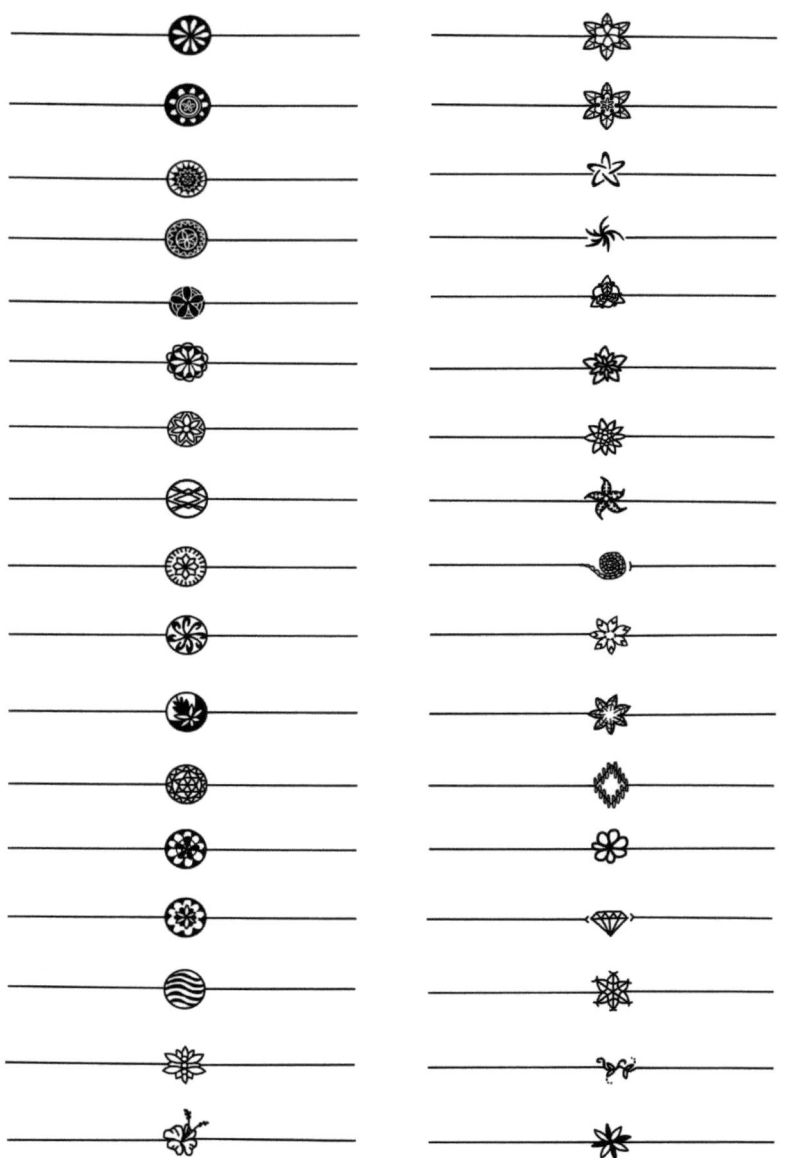

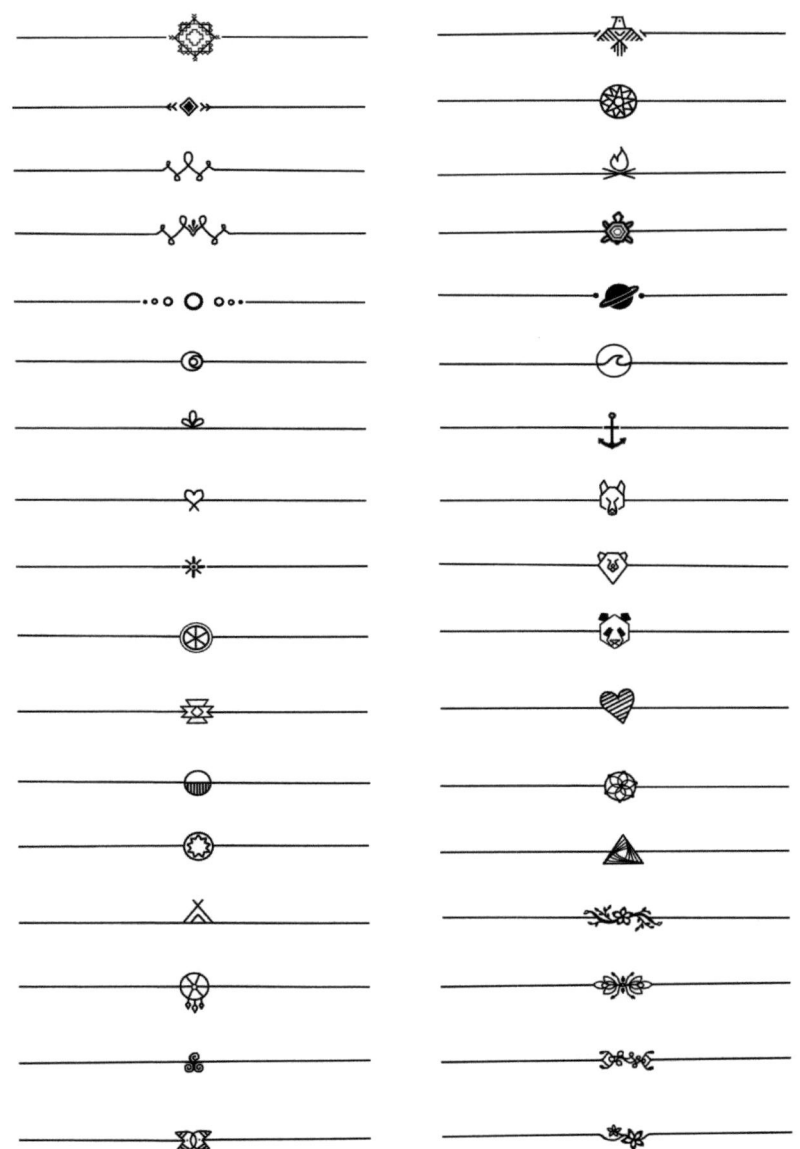

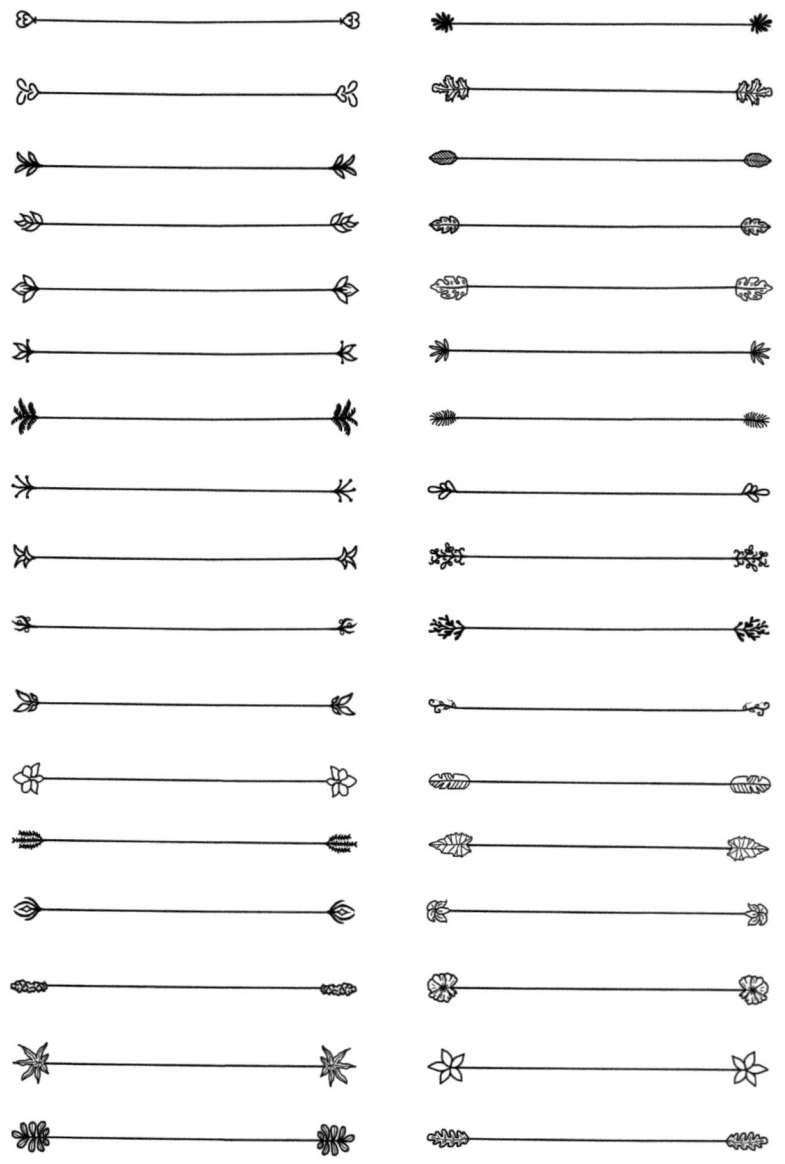

18

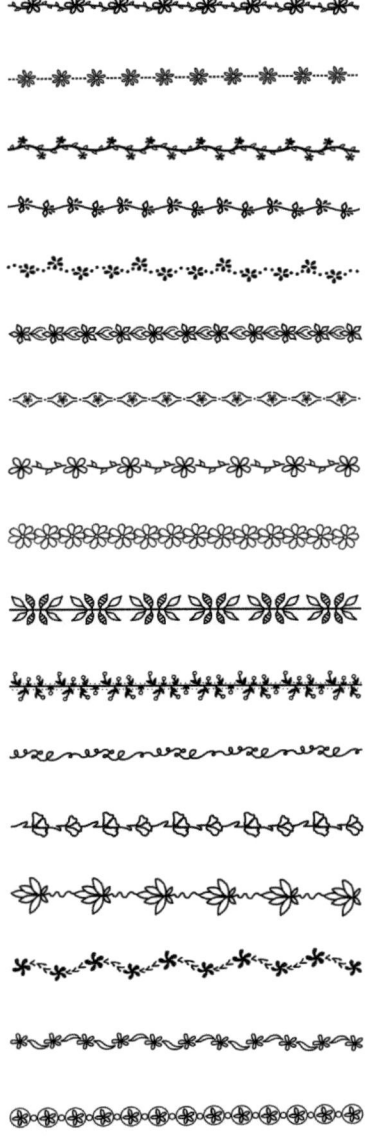

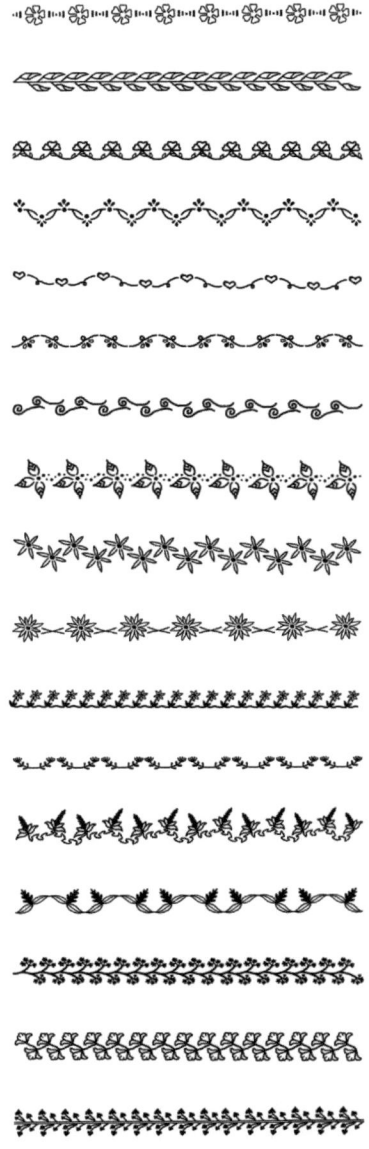

19

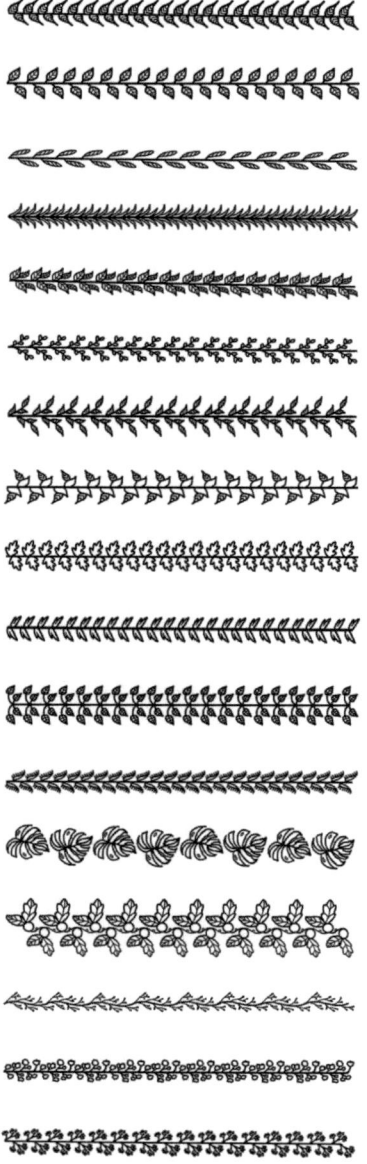

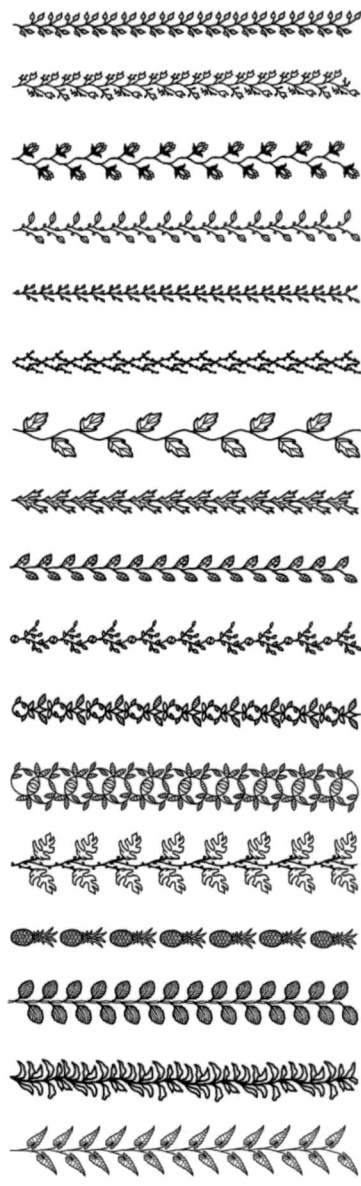

20

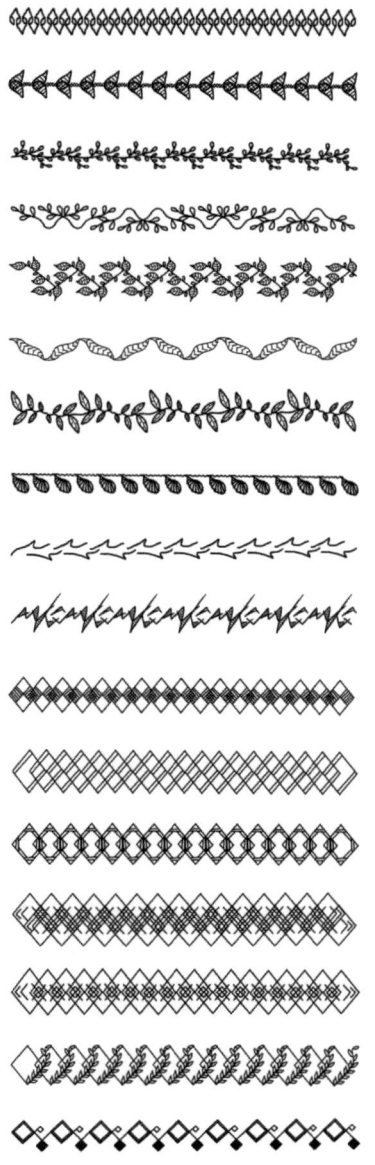
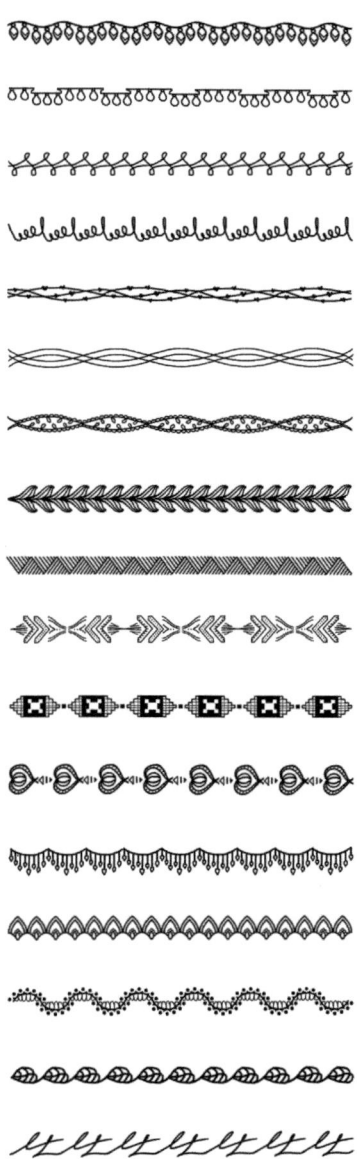

21

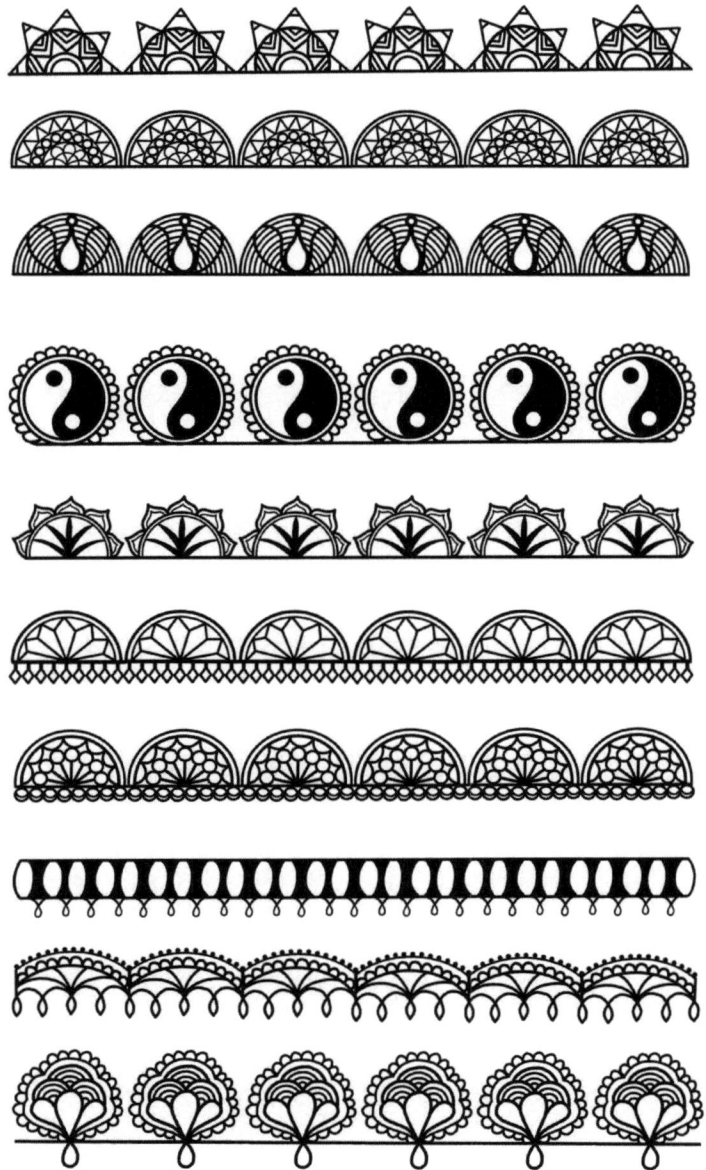

23

24

25

27

29

Habit trackers

☒ done
☐ not done

	1	2	3	4	5	6	7	8	9	10	11	12	13	14	15
	16	17	18	19	20	21	22	23	24	25	26	27	28	29	30
cleaning															
no sugar															
Netflix															
bed by 10pm															
up by 8am															
time outside															
spent money															
music															
meet friends															
bullet journal															
cooking															
stretching															
reading															
do a hobby															
skincare															
meal prep															
vitamins															
IG post															
workout															
hair wash															
water plants															

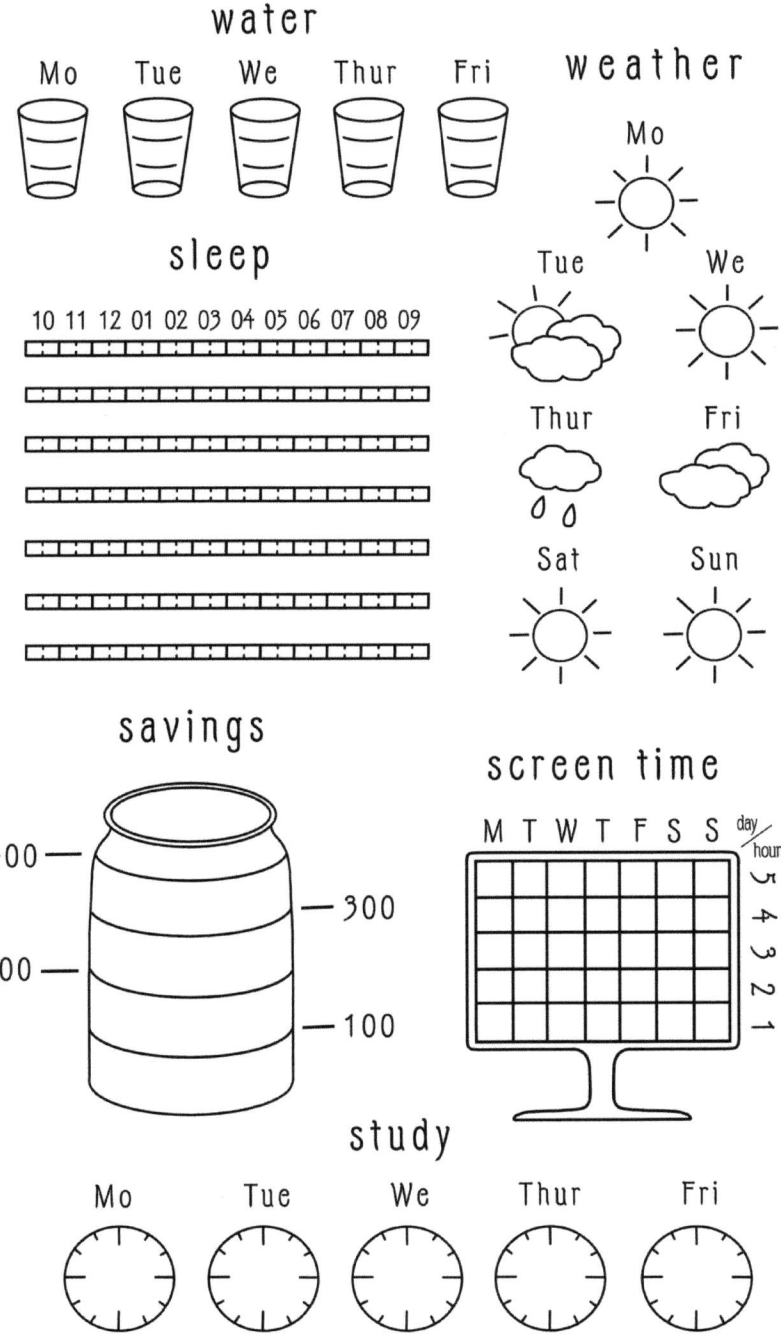

Banners

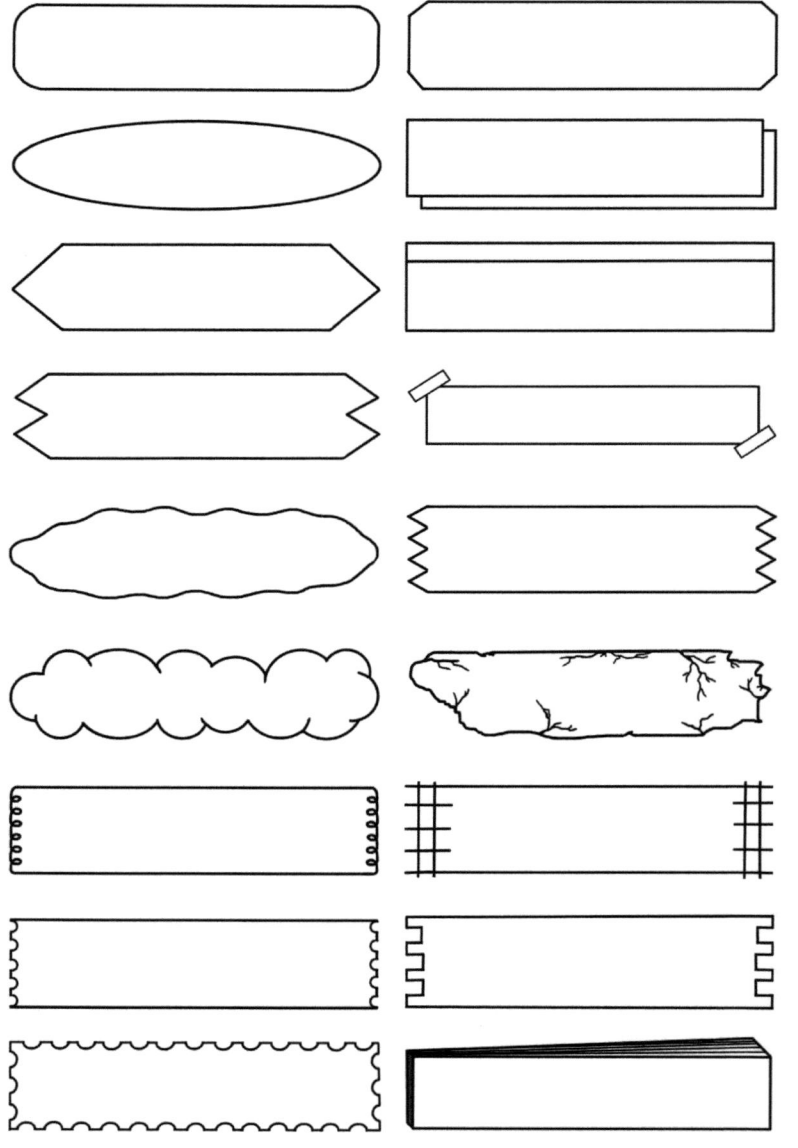

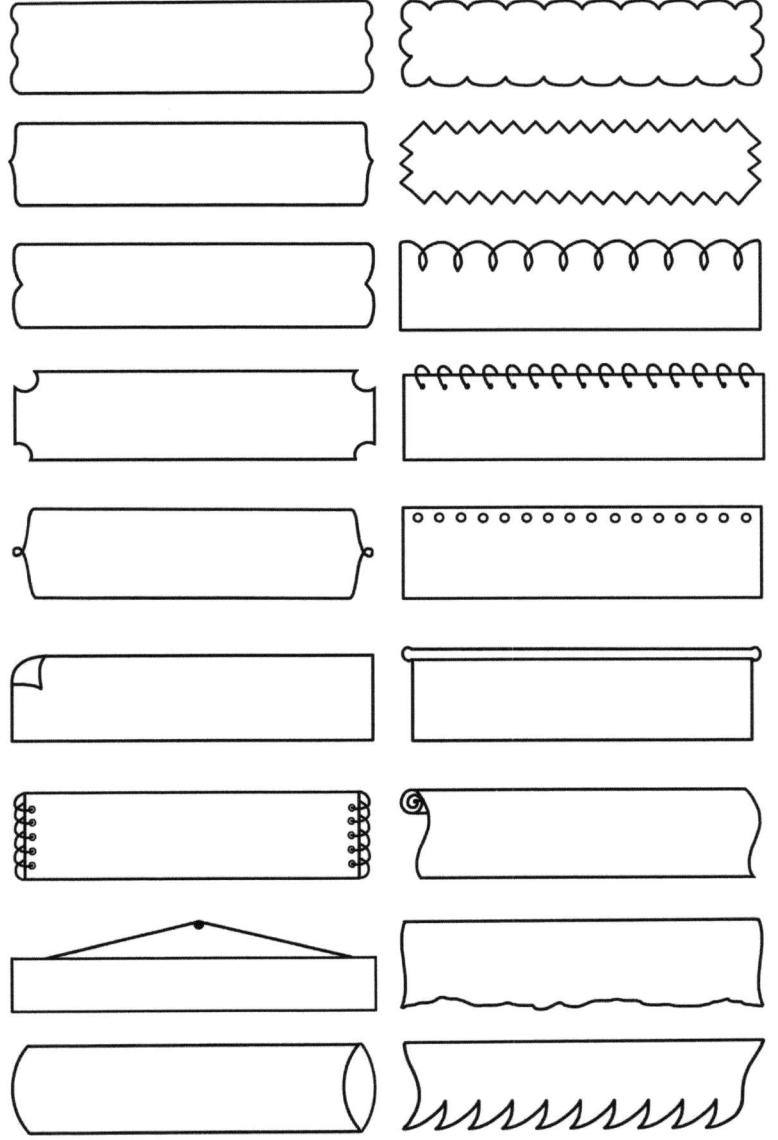

35

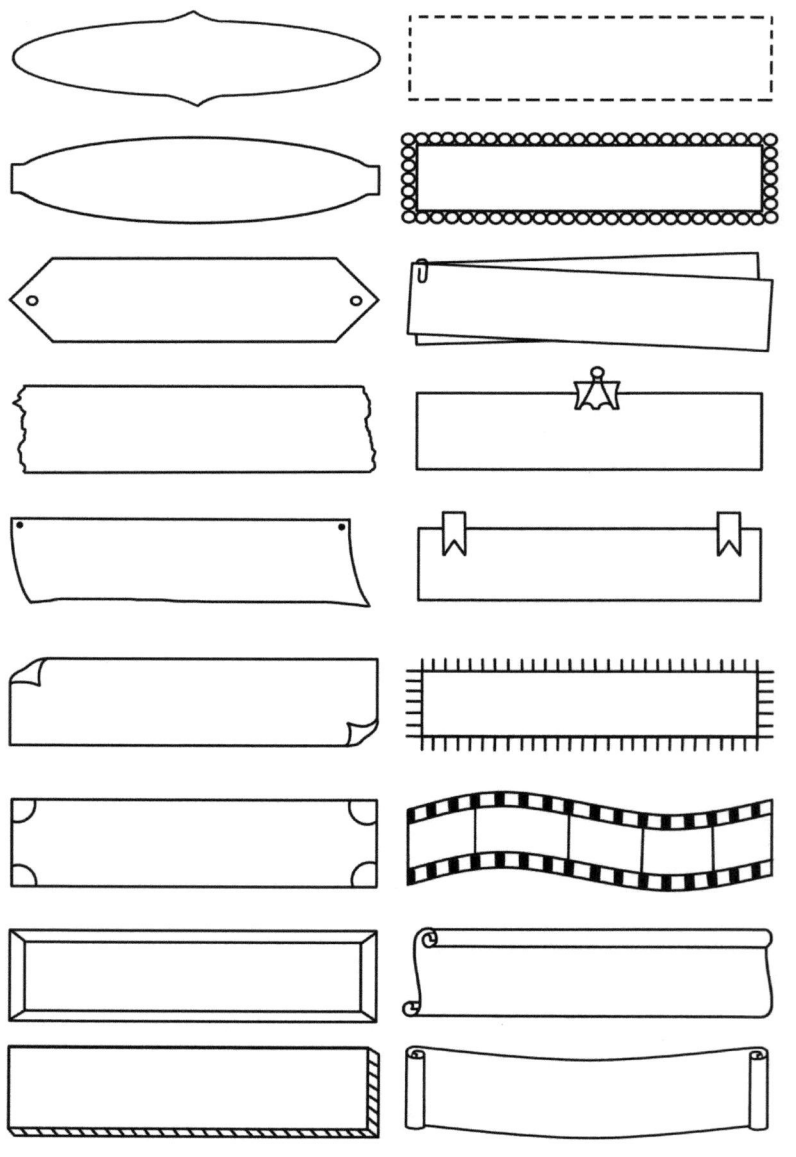

36

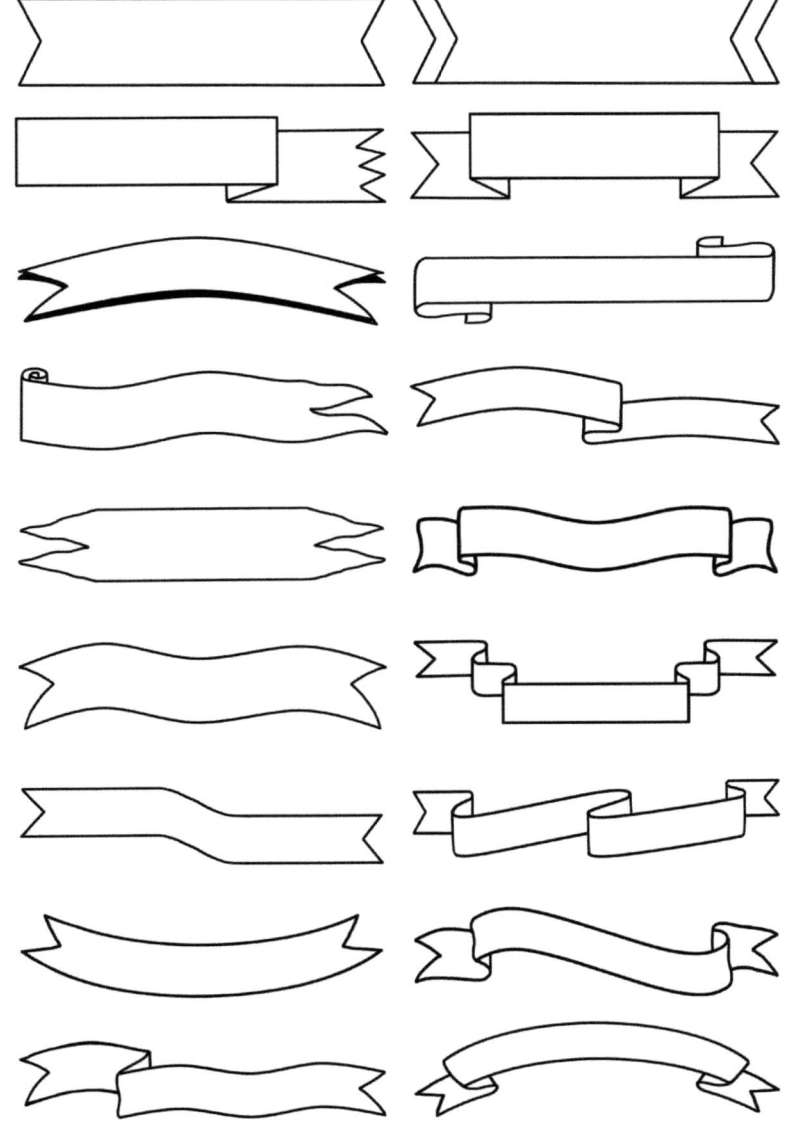

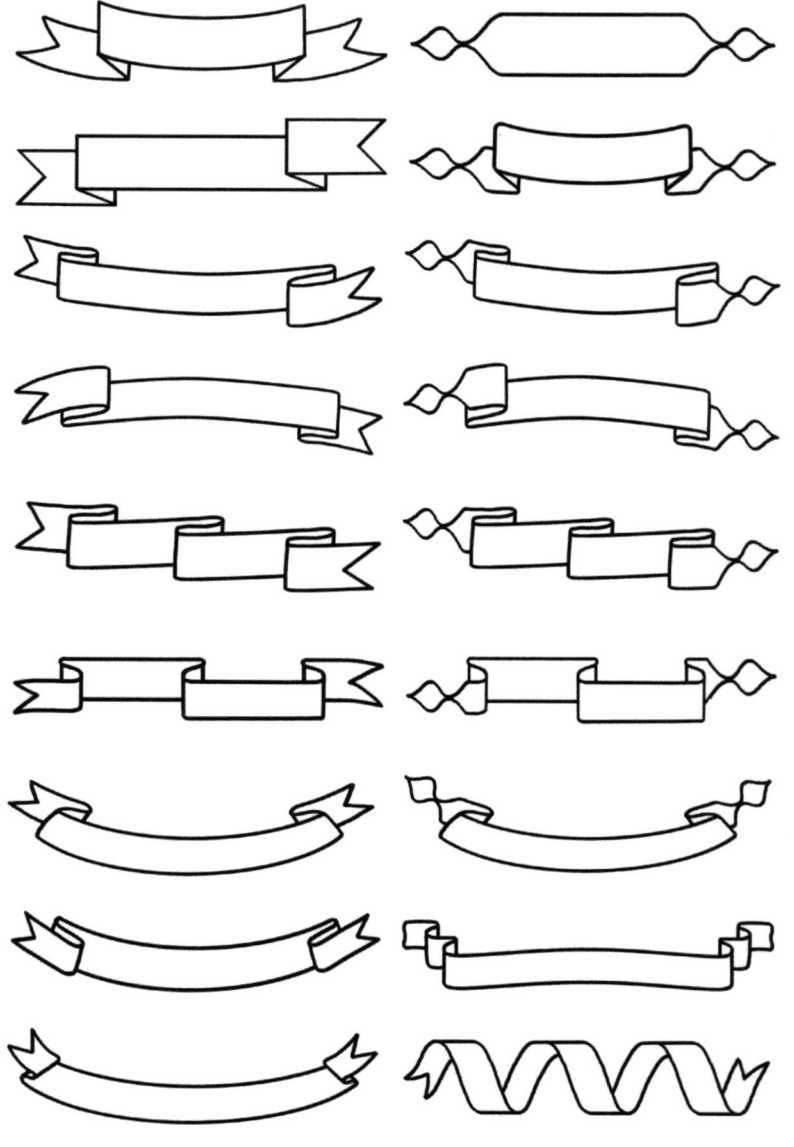

38

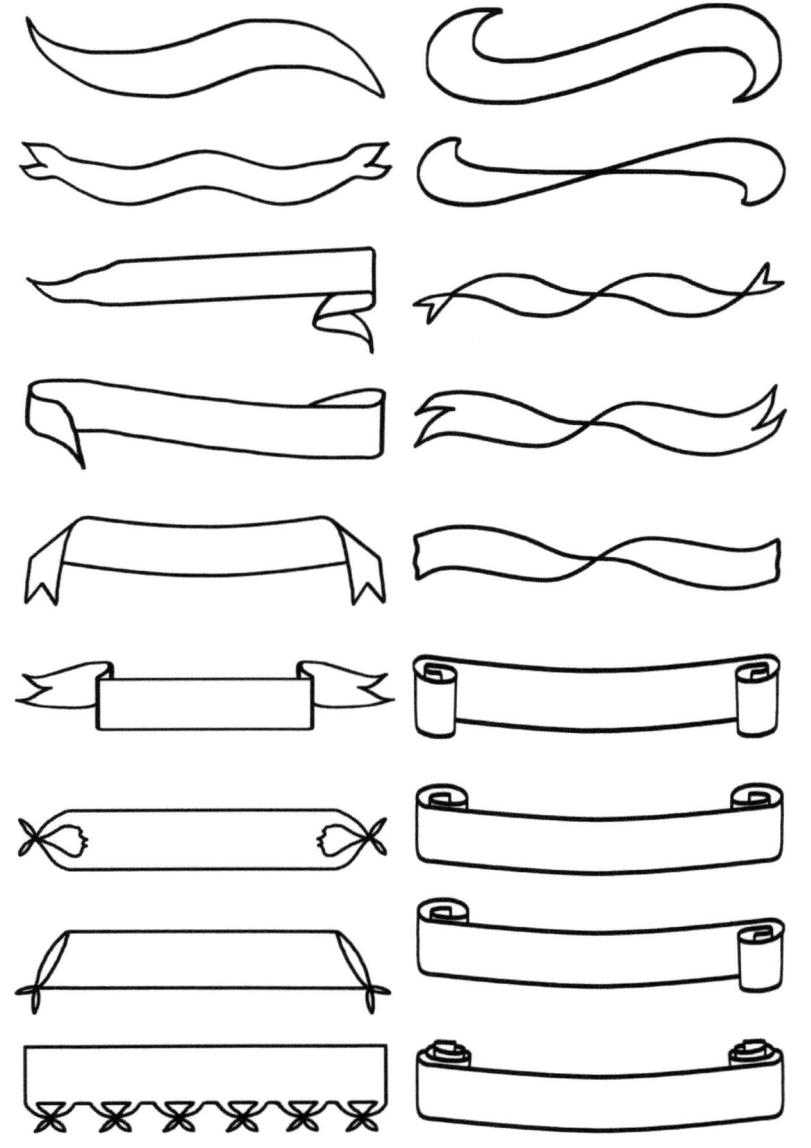

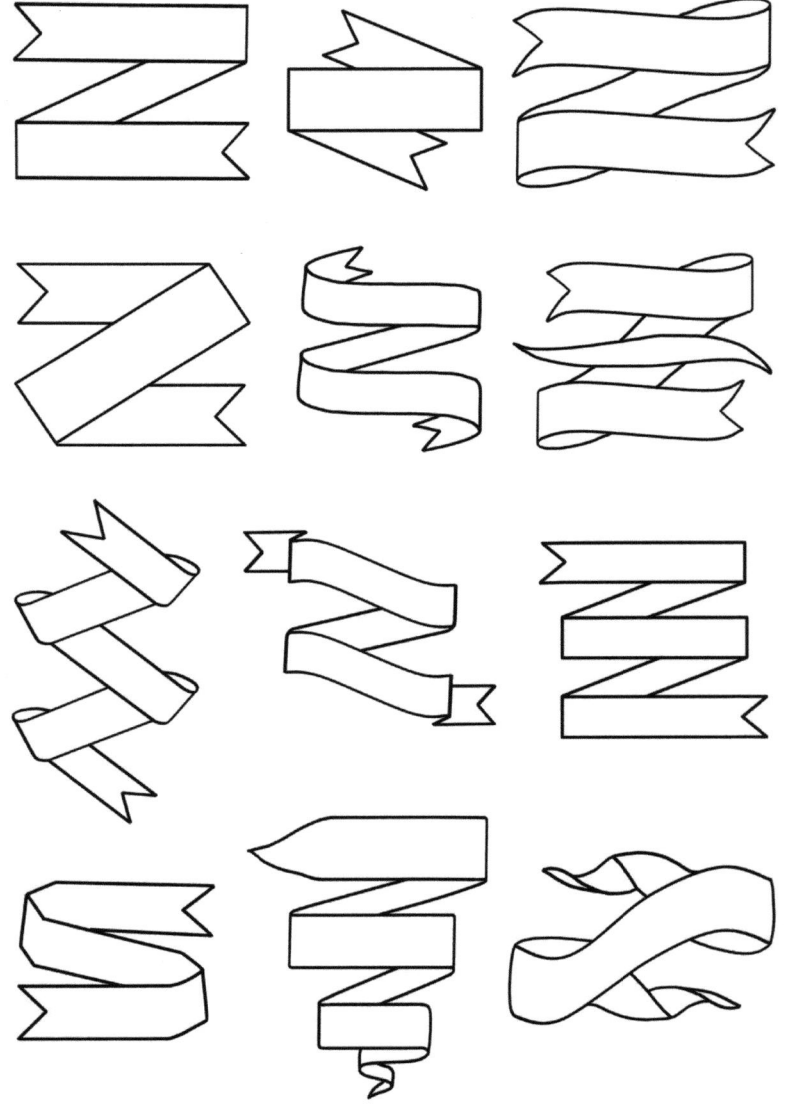

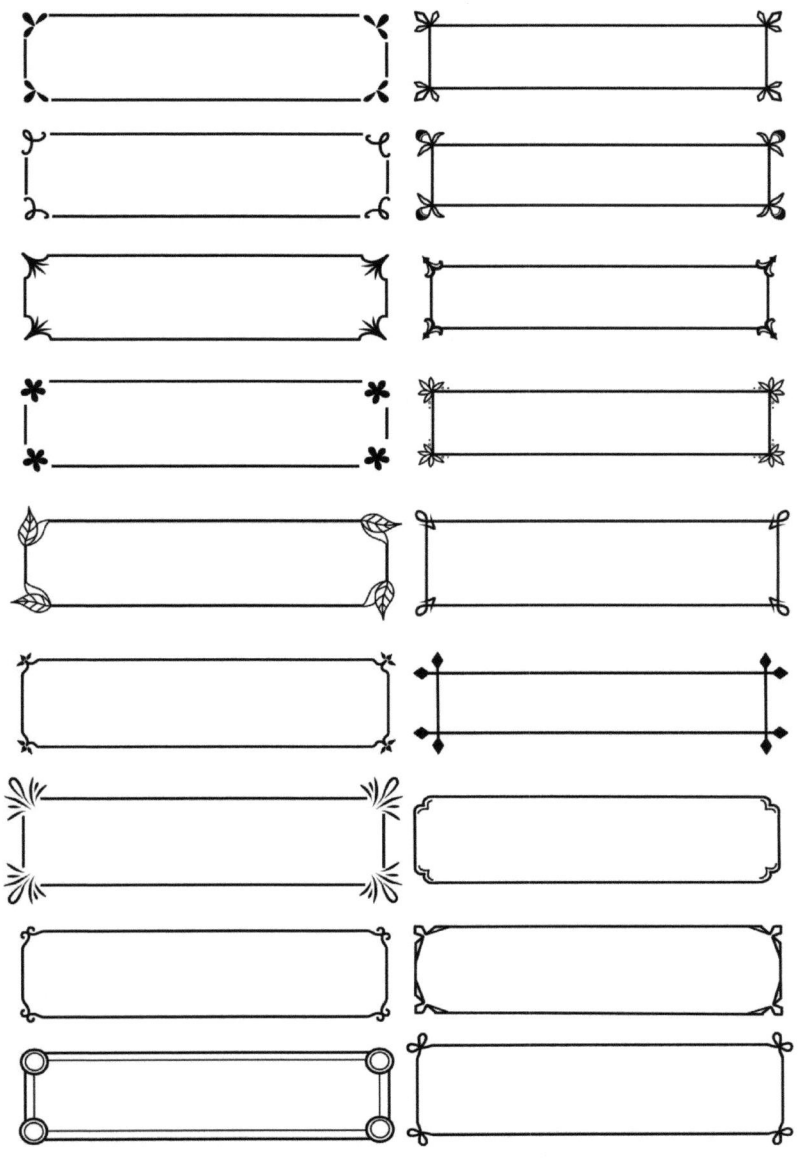

41

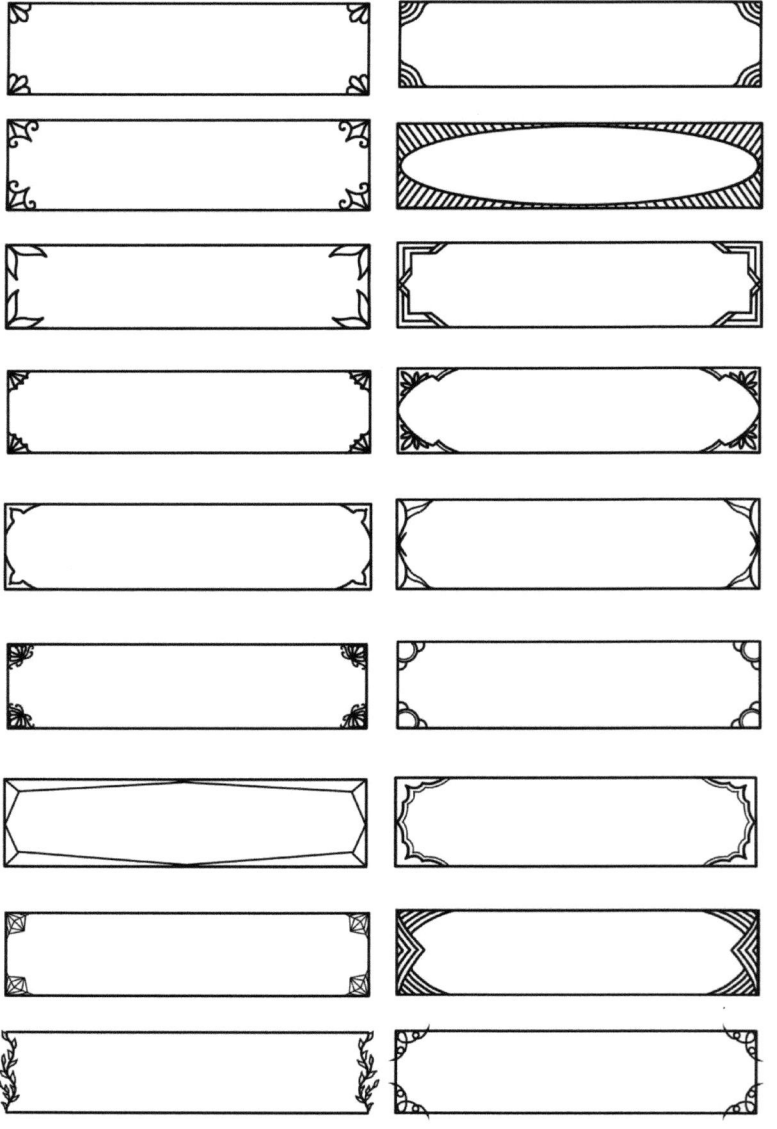

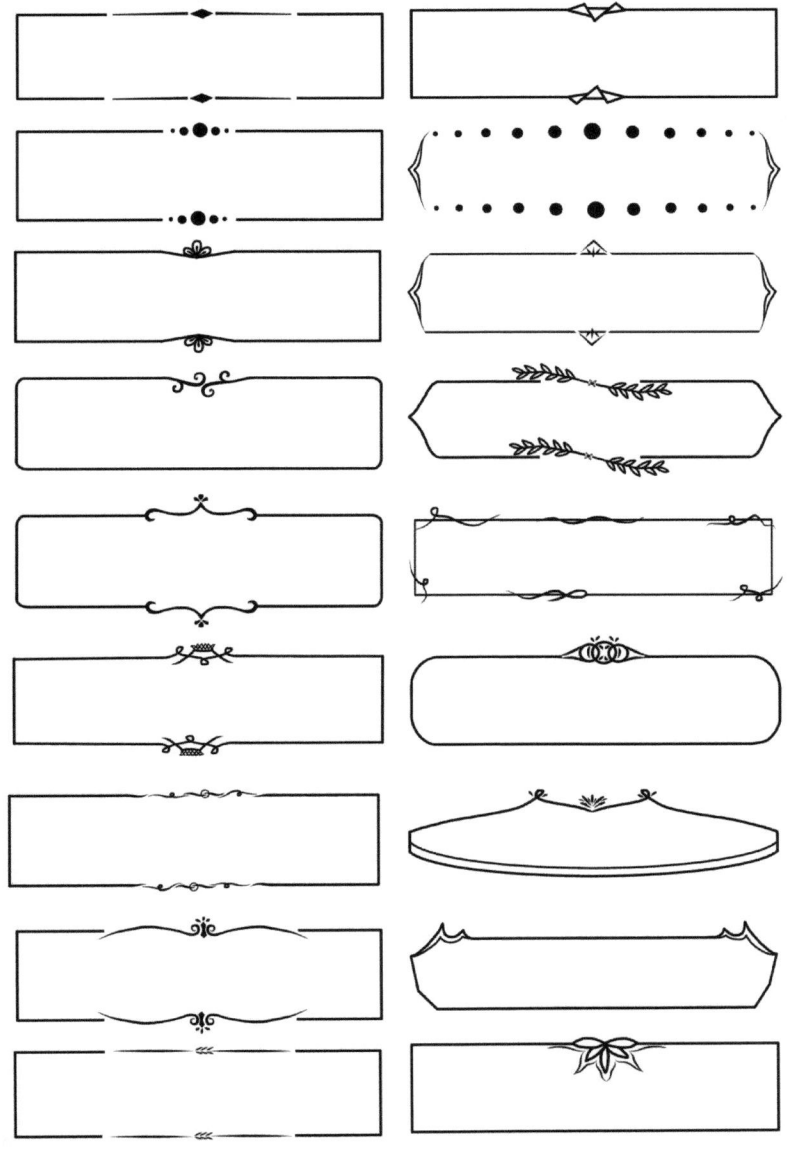

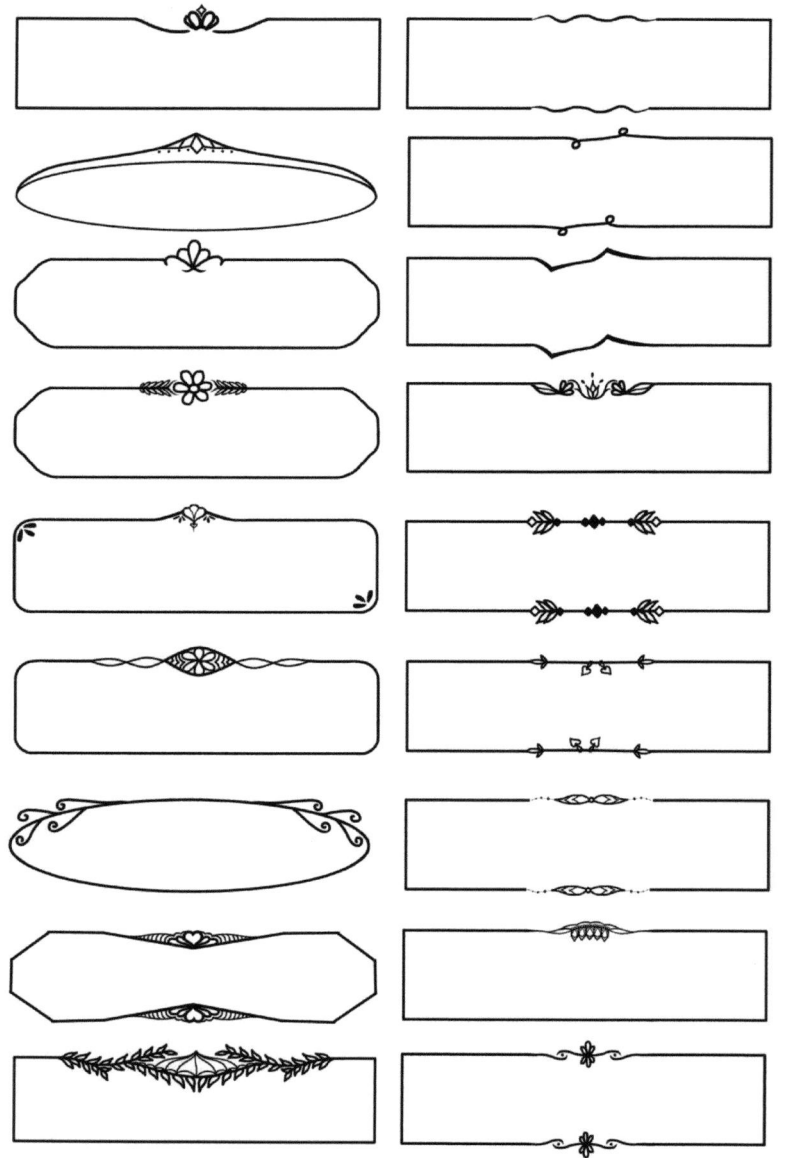

44

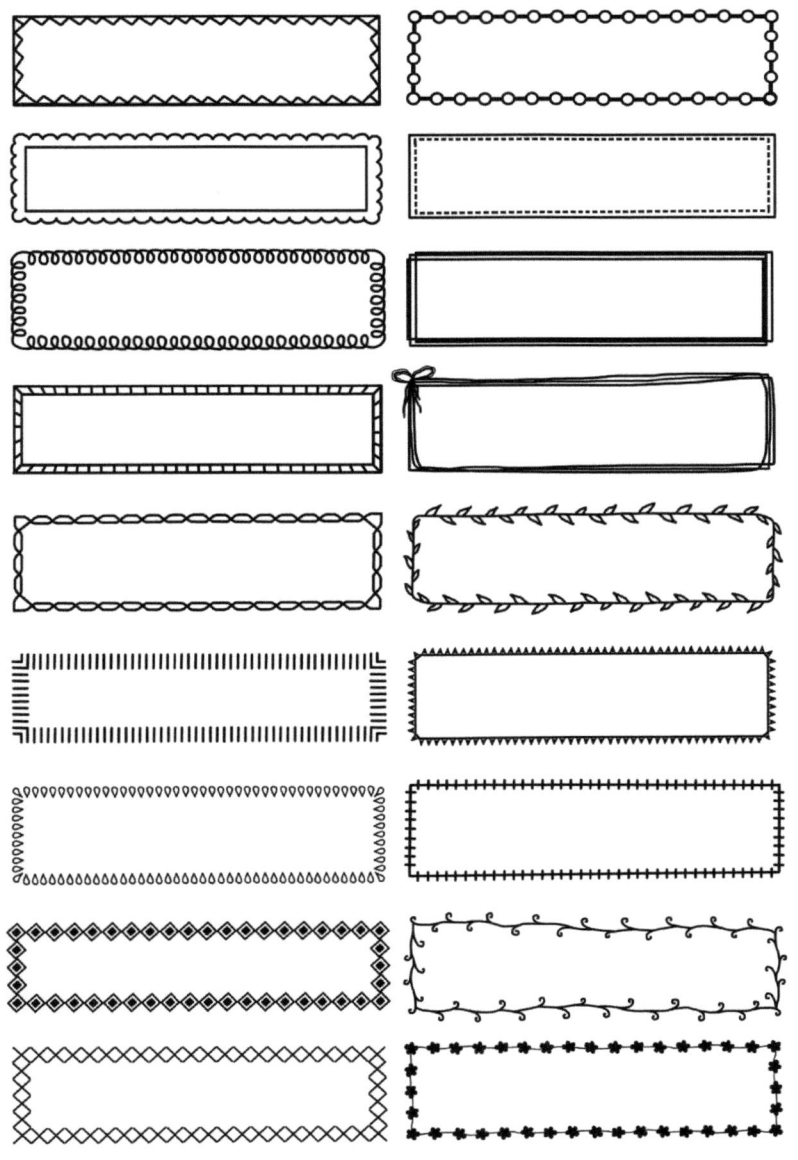

45

Mood trackers

- 🟨 happy
- 🟡 good
- 🟧 stressed
- 🟥 sad

mood board
autumn

sweater weather

cozy season

reading books is like
exploring another world

Circles

50

51

53

54

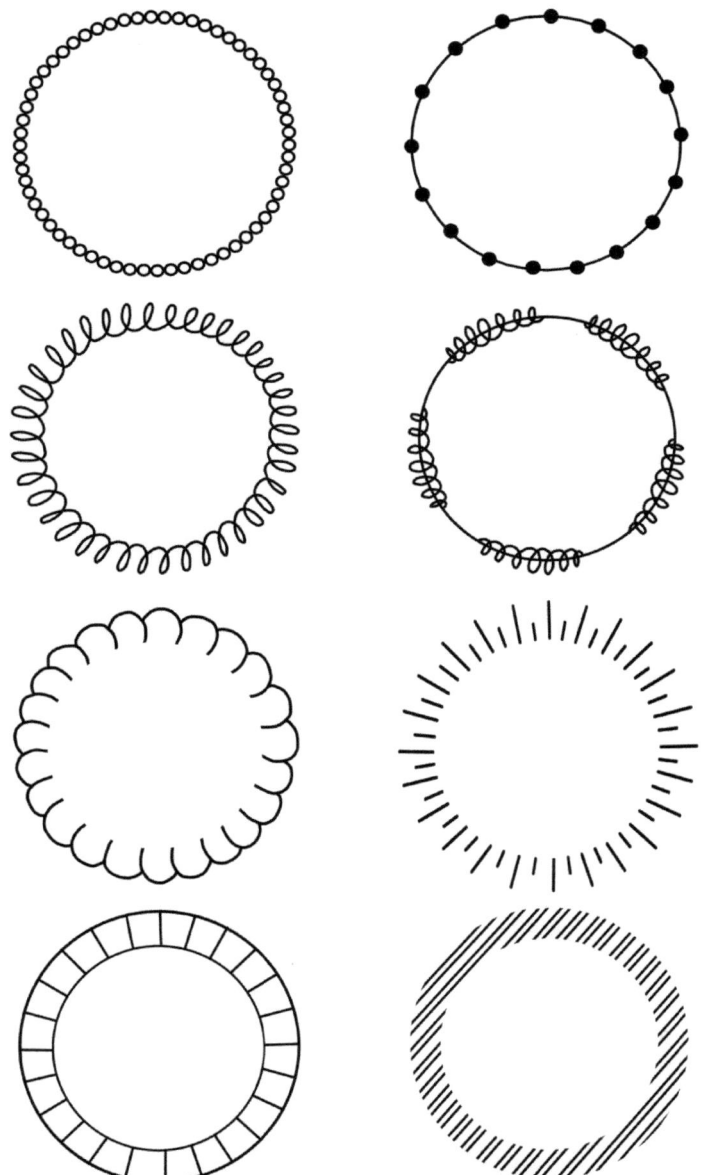

55

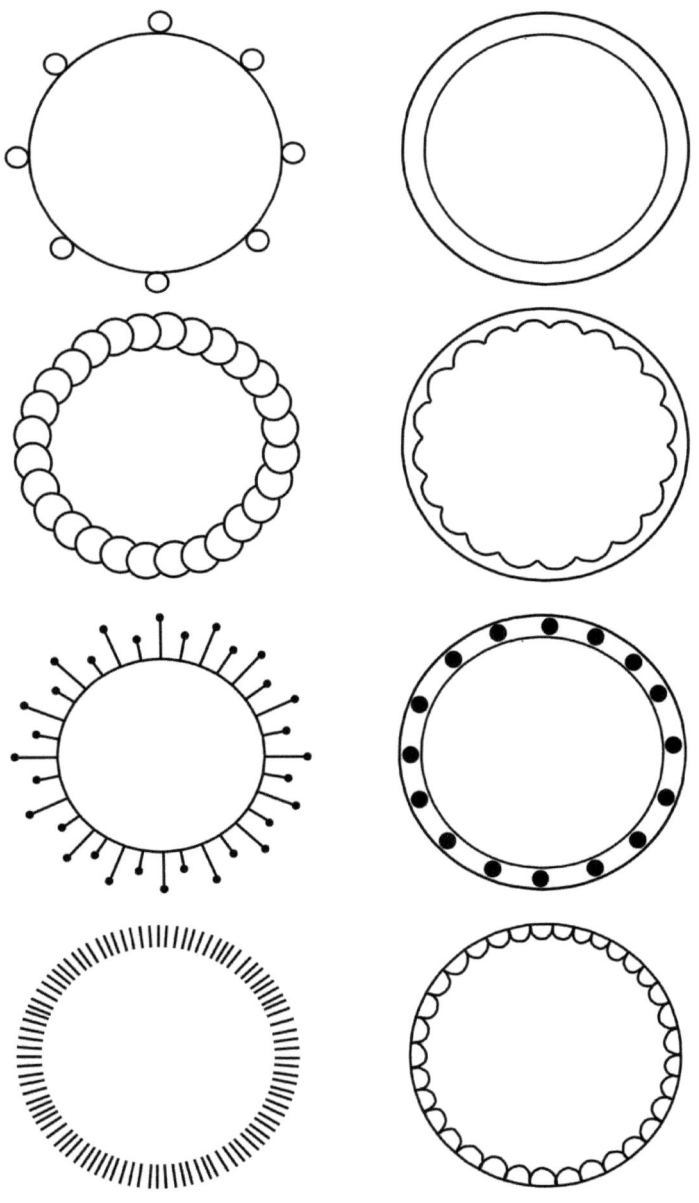

57

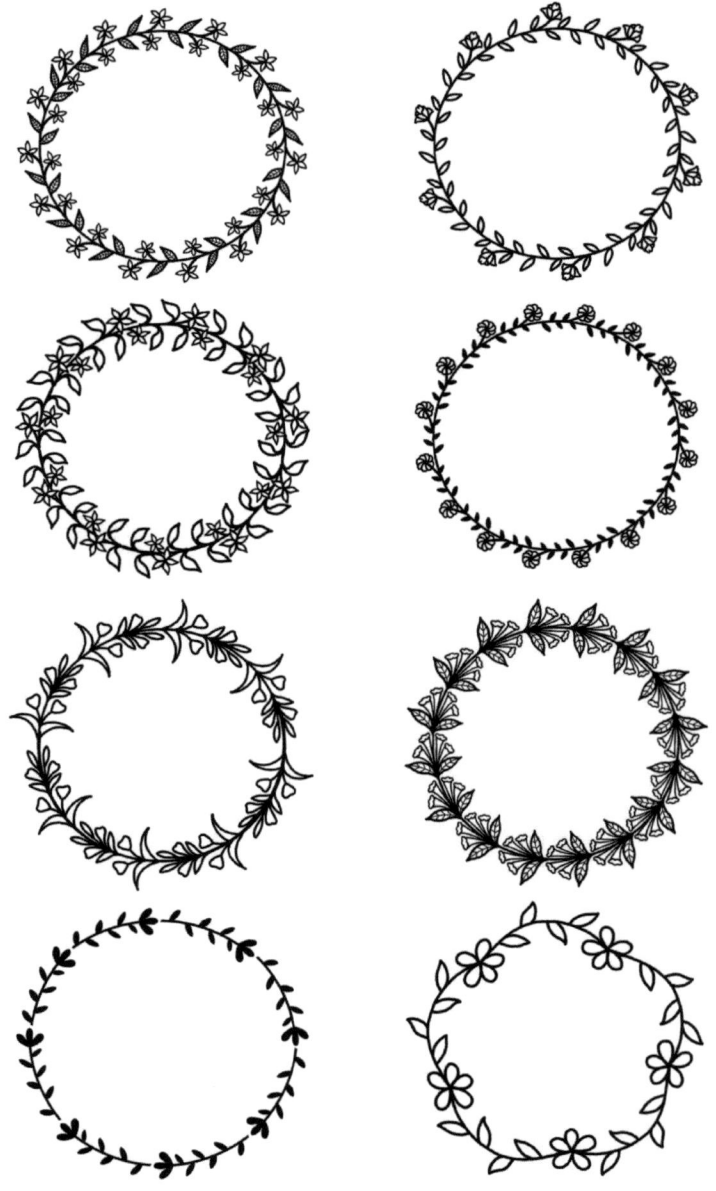

58

59

60

from

to

Monday

Tuesday

notes

Wednesday

notes

Thursday

notes

Friday

notes

Weekend

thankful for

bucket list

my plans

goals

expectations

reflections

Corners

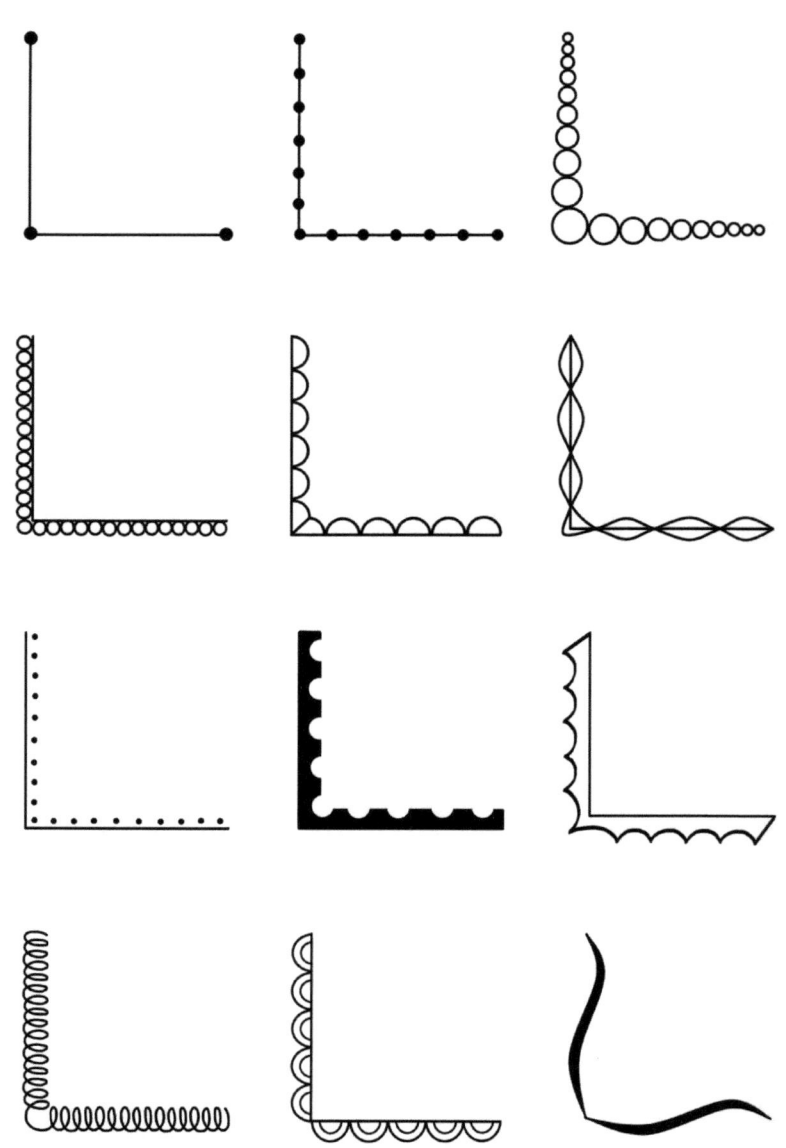

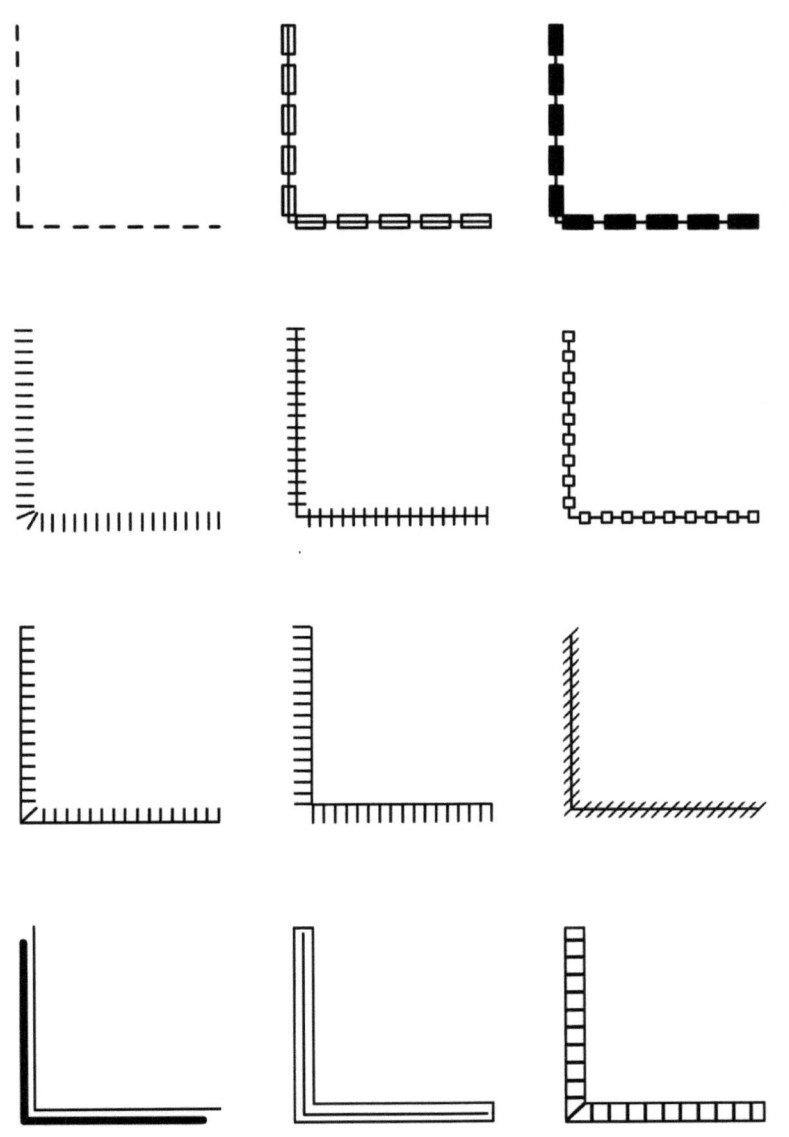

67

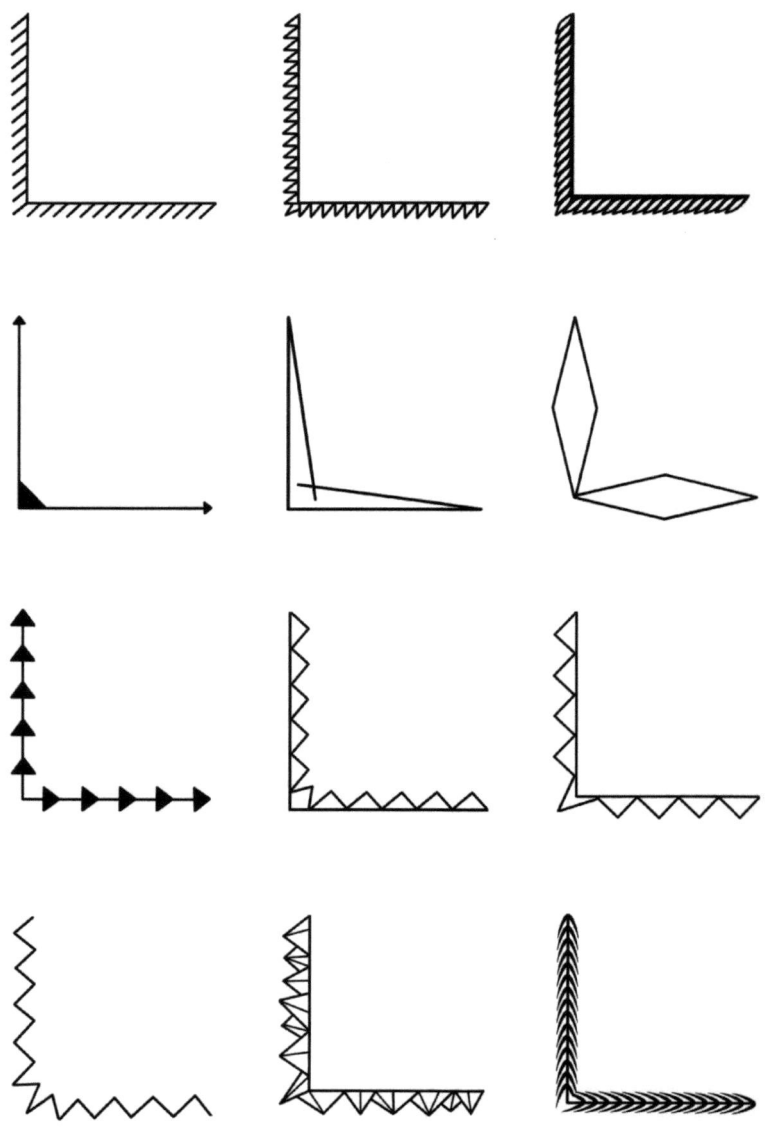

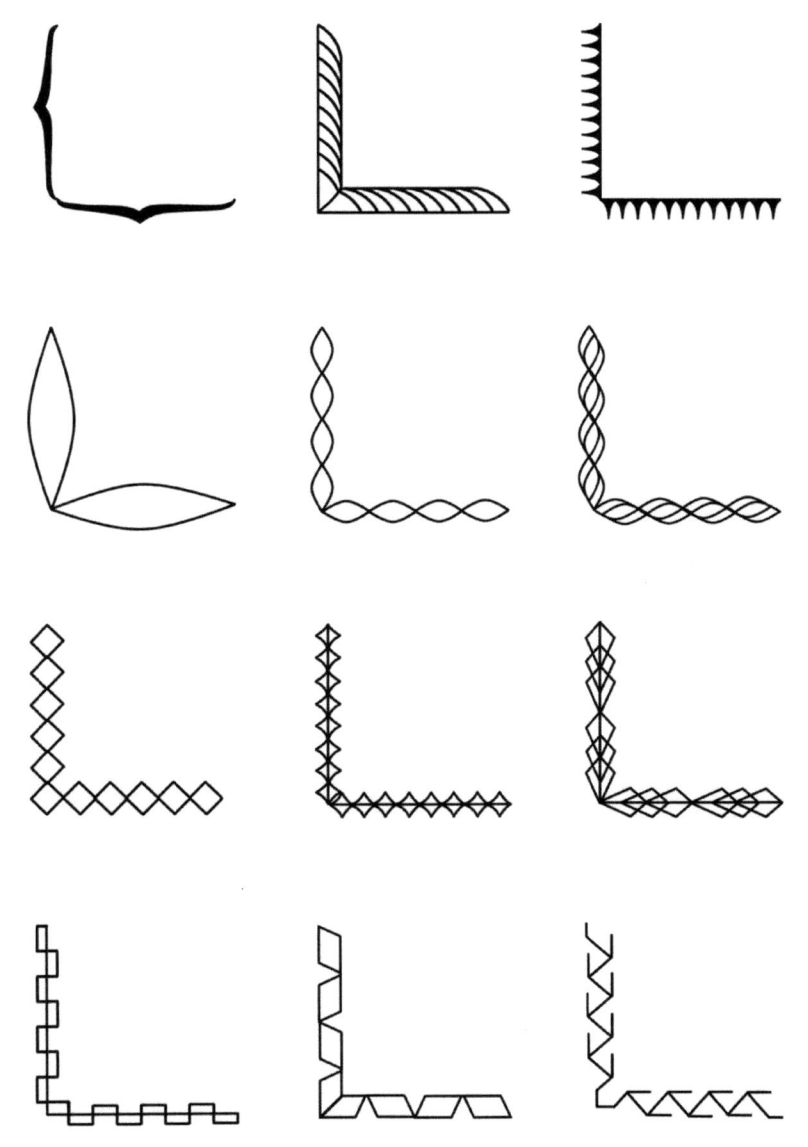

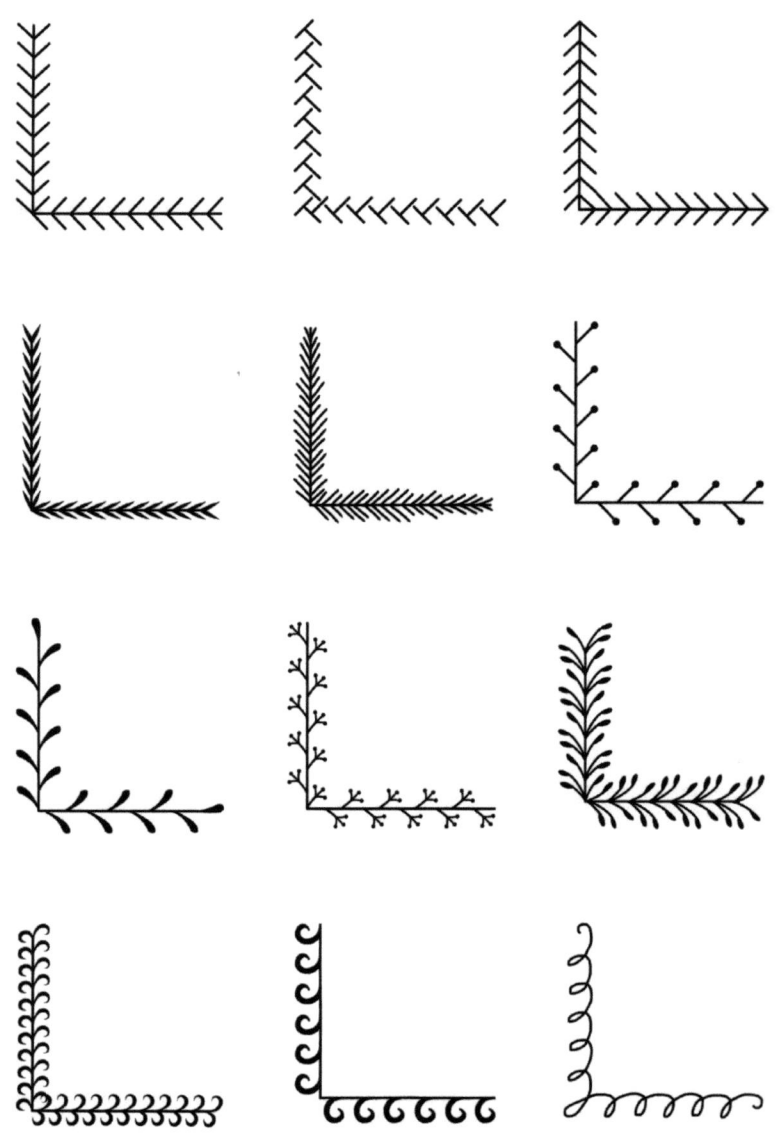

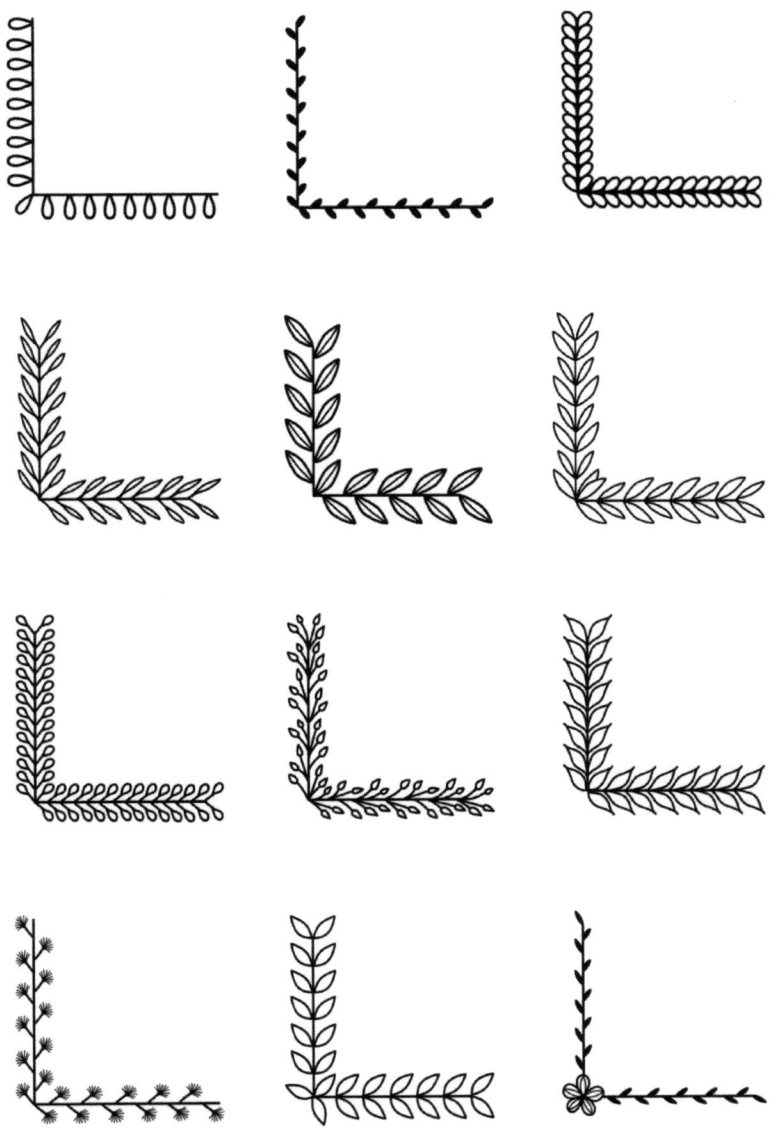

71

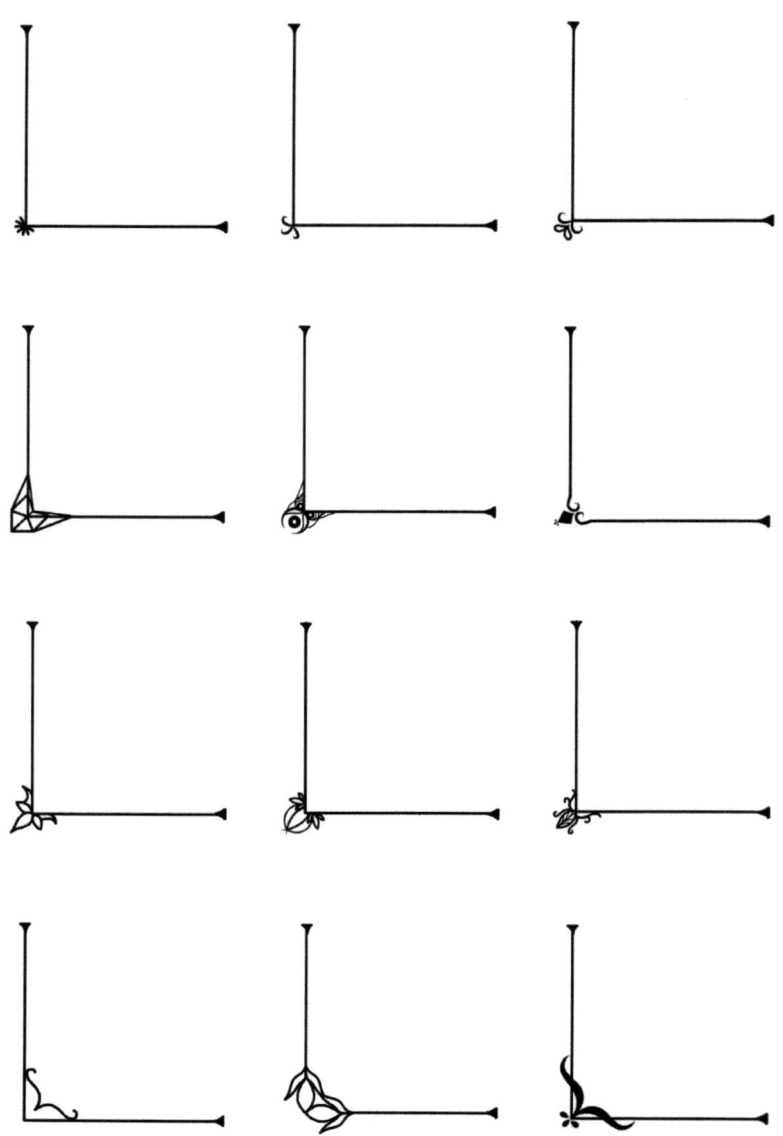

72

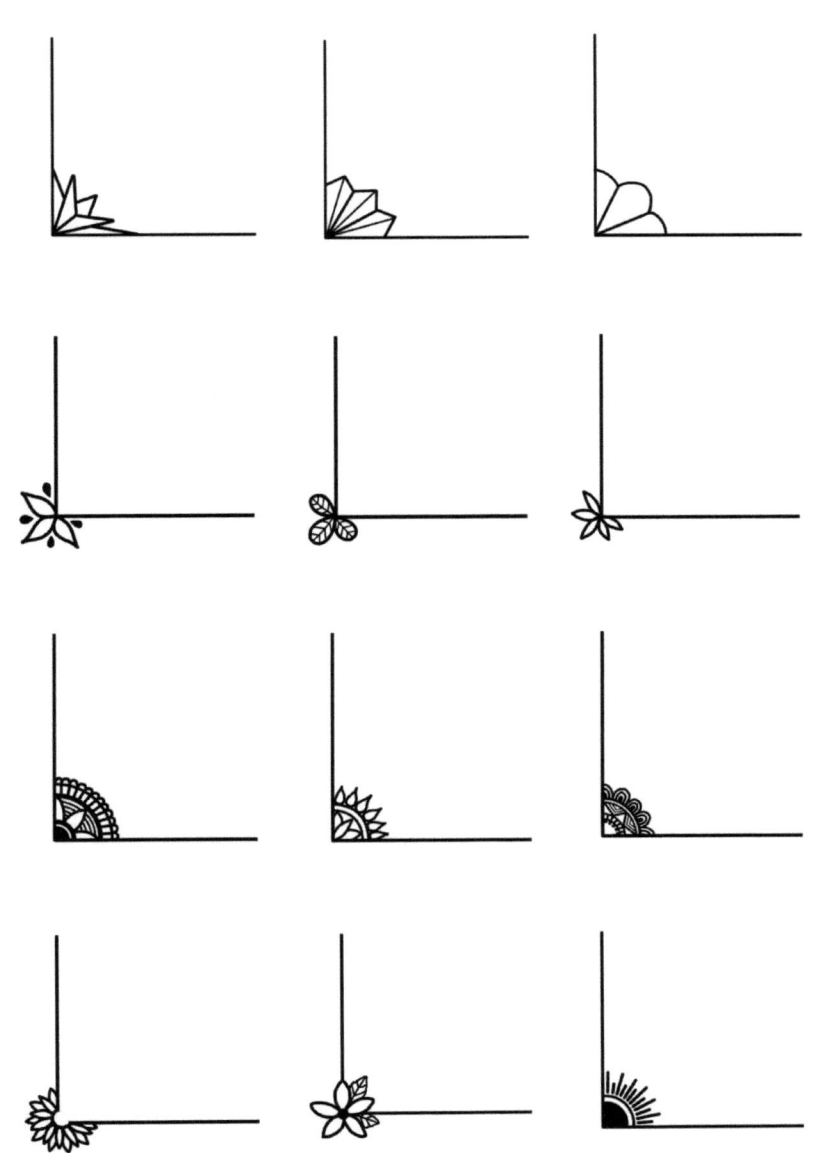

73

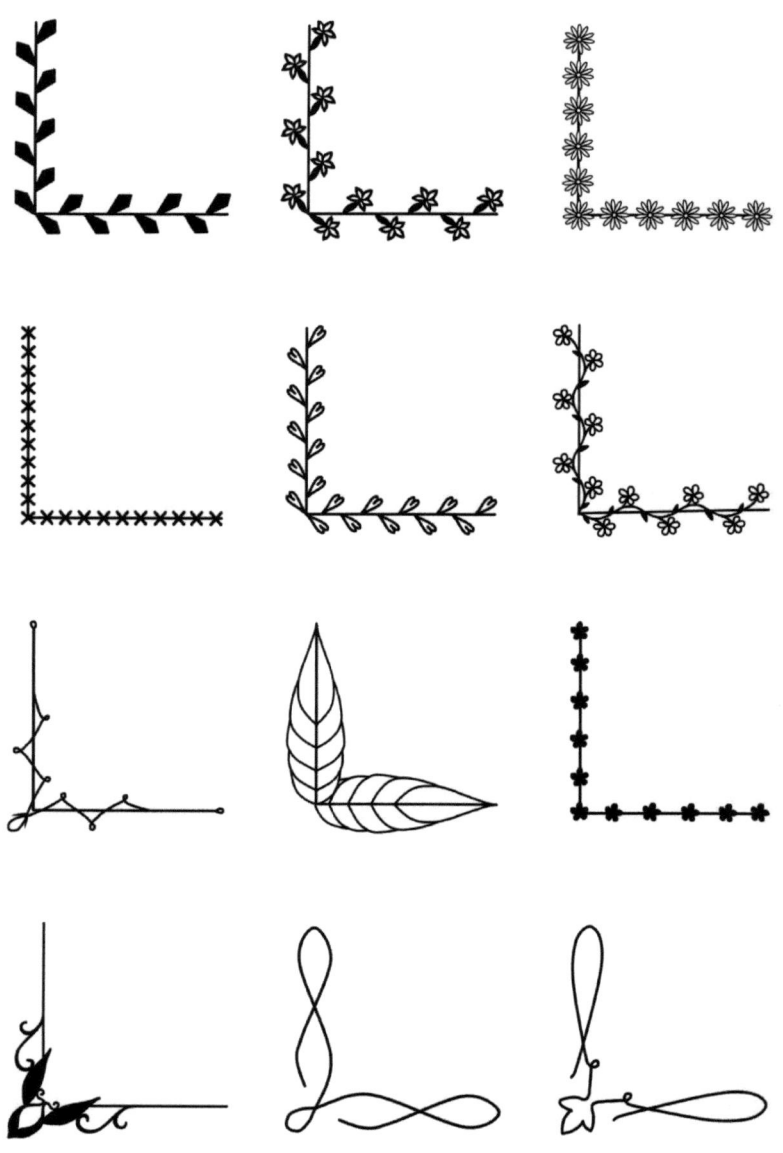

74

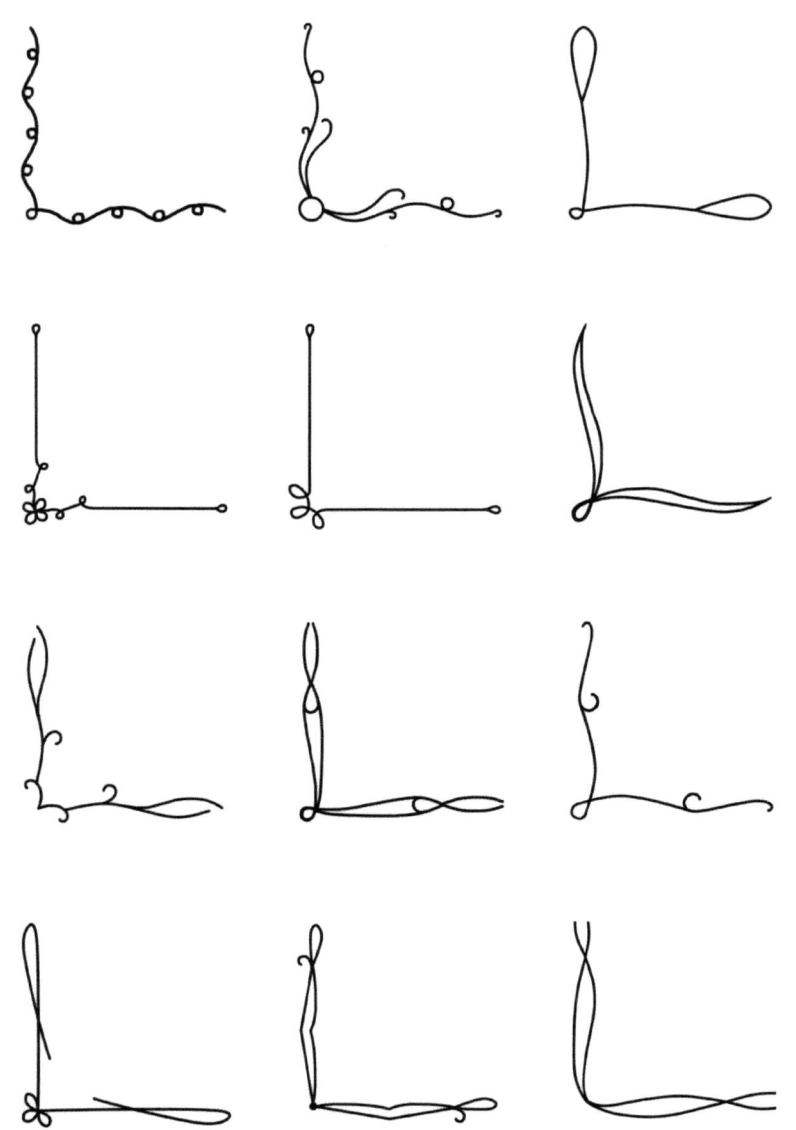

75

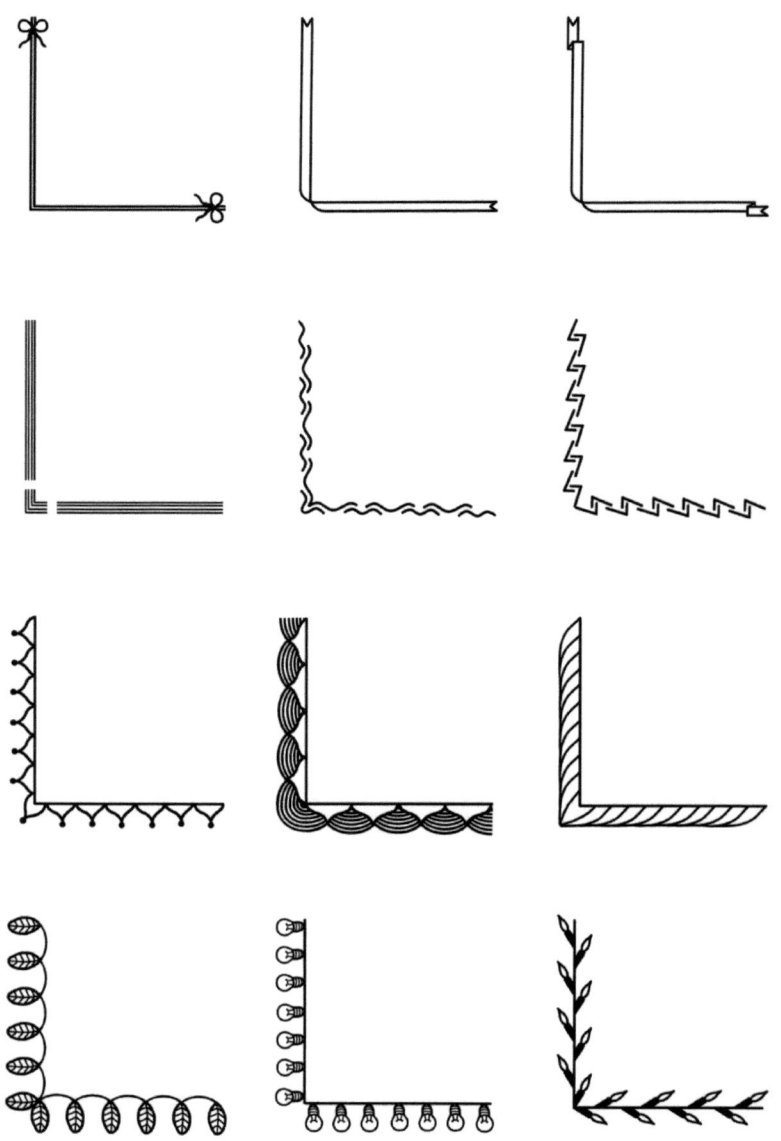

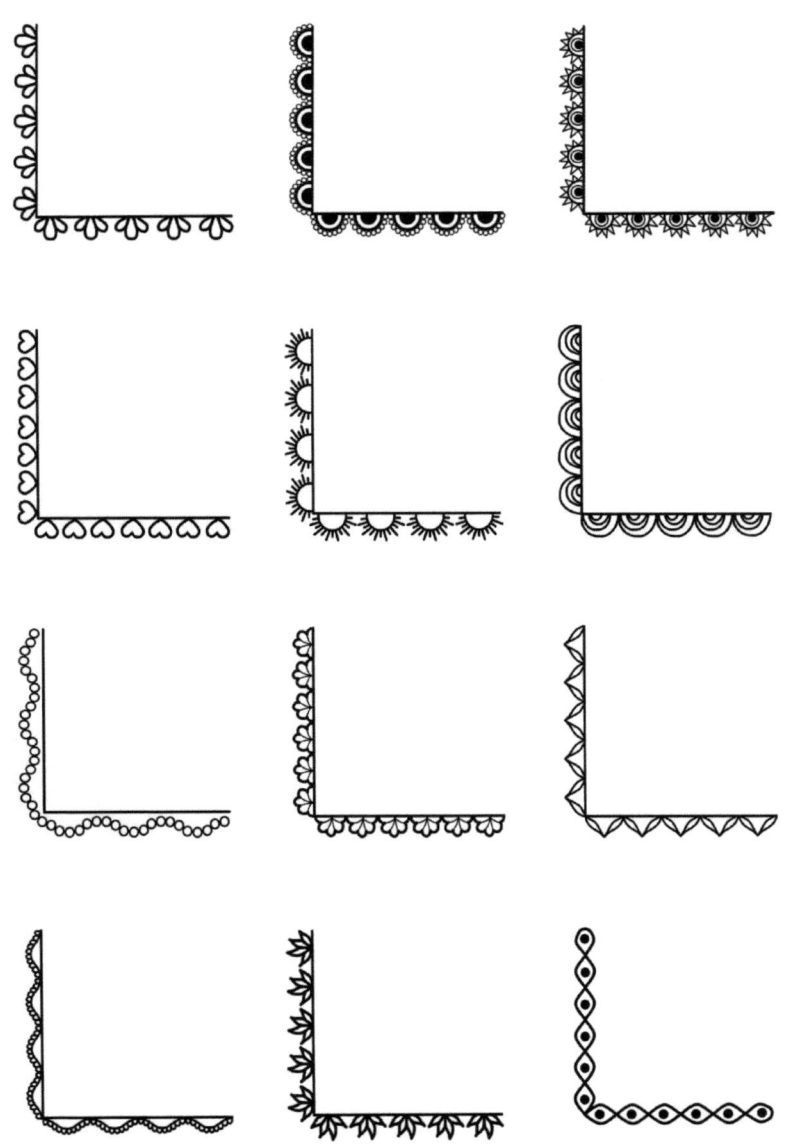

About the holidays

"traveling
is my life

statue of liberty
statue of liberty
statue of liberty
statue of liberty
statue of liberty
statue of liberty
statue of liberty
statue of liberty
statue of liberty
statue of liberty
statue of liberty
statue of liberty
statue of liberty
statue of liberty
statue of liberty
statue of liberty
tatue of liberty
statue of liberty
statue of liberty
statue of liberty
stat

NEW
YORK

beach
city

July

M	T	W	T	F	S	S
				1	2	3	4	5	6
7	8	9	10	11	12	13
14	15	16	17	18	19	20
21	22	23	24	25	26	27
28	29	30	31			

goals

- be happy
- making memories
- ____

events

- festival
- open air
- travel to Italy
- ____

@alohaa_jana

@alohaa_jana

@janinars

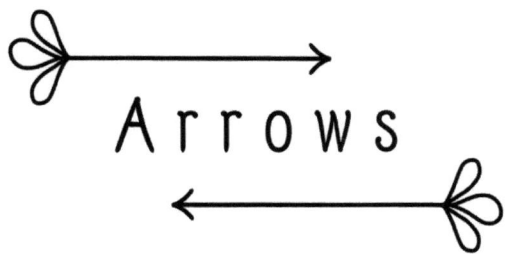

Arrows

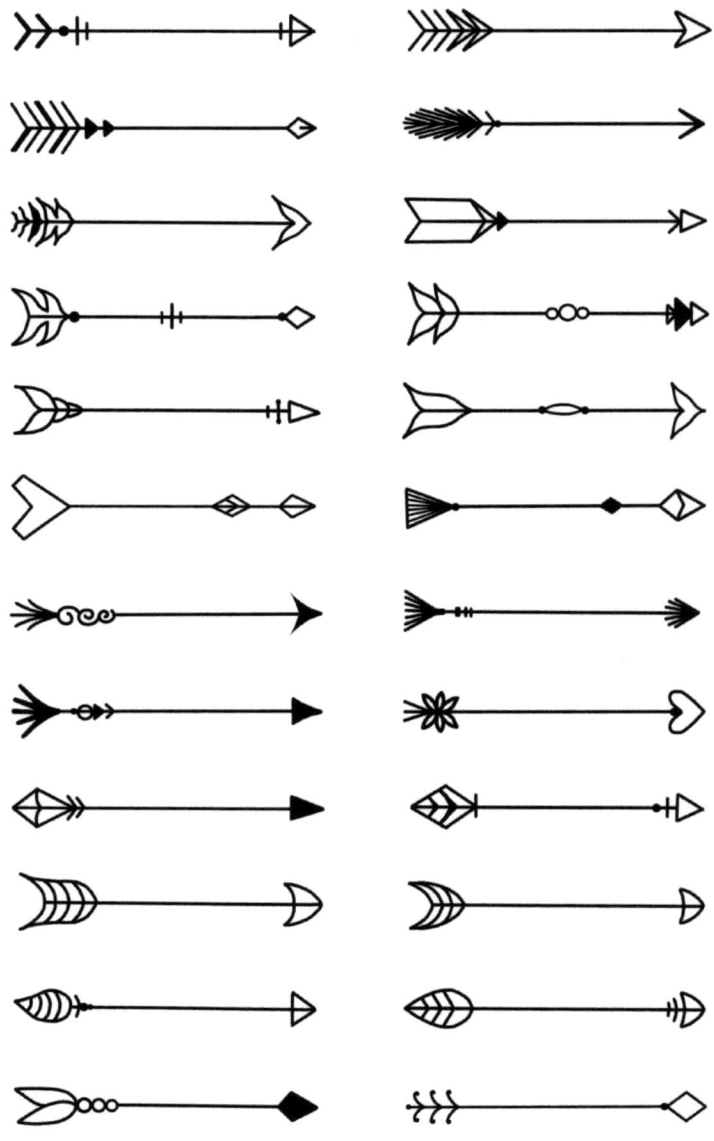

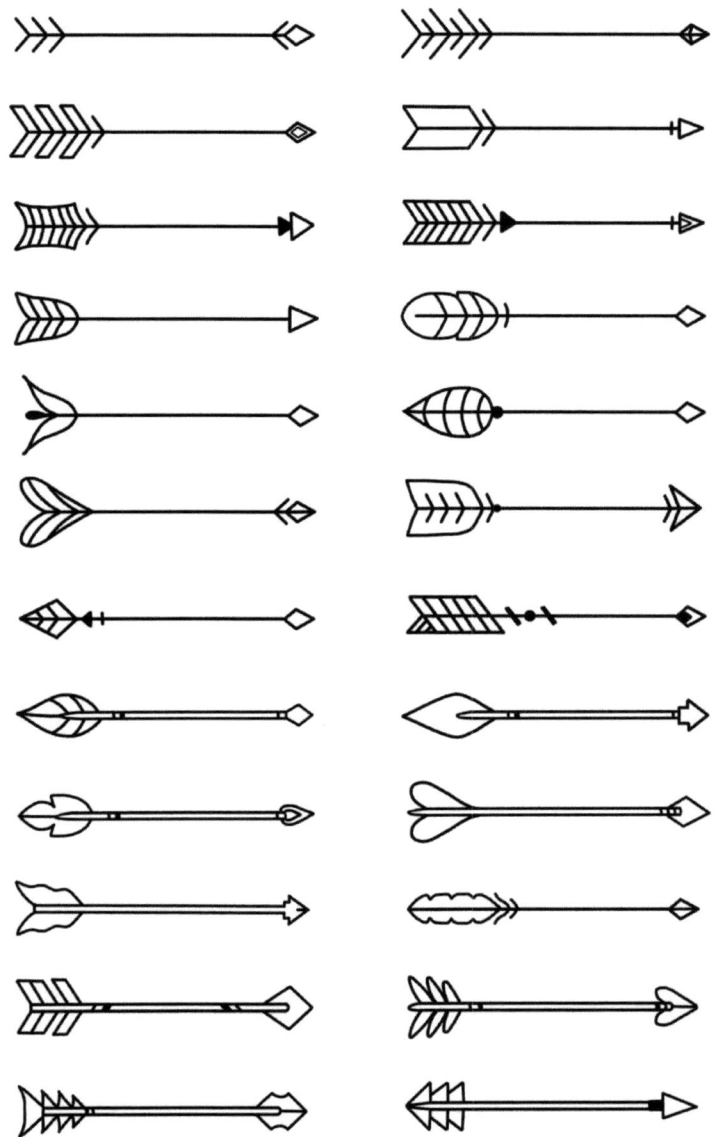

83

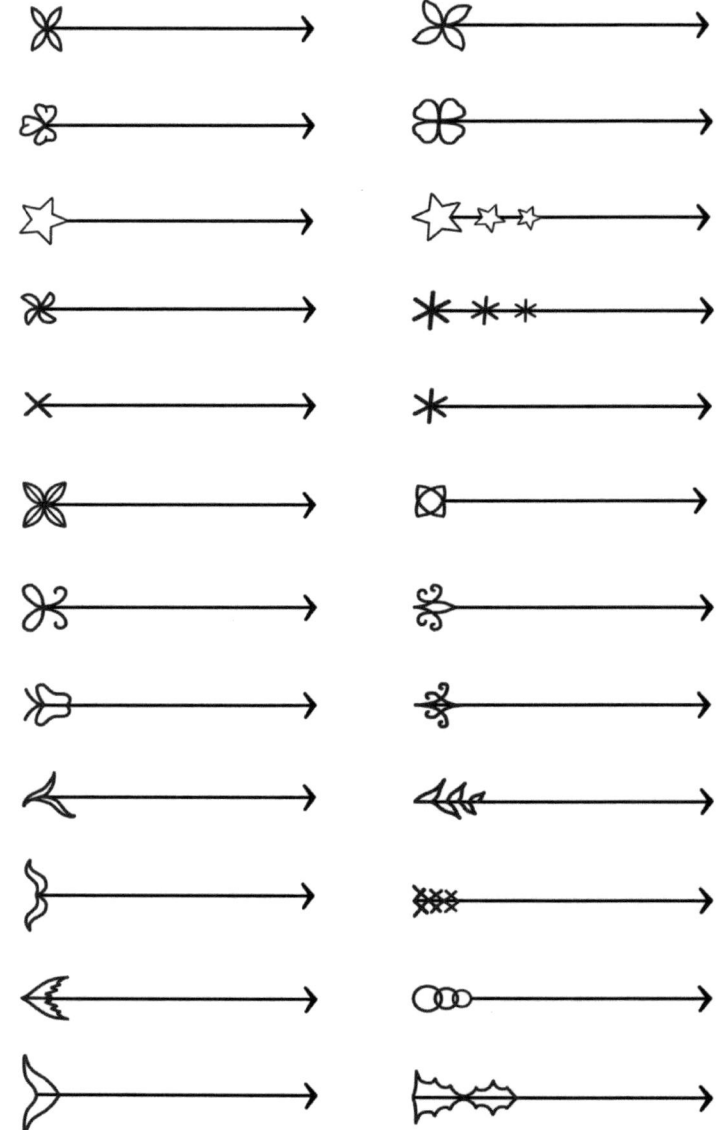

84

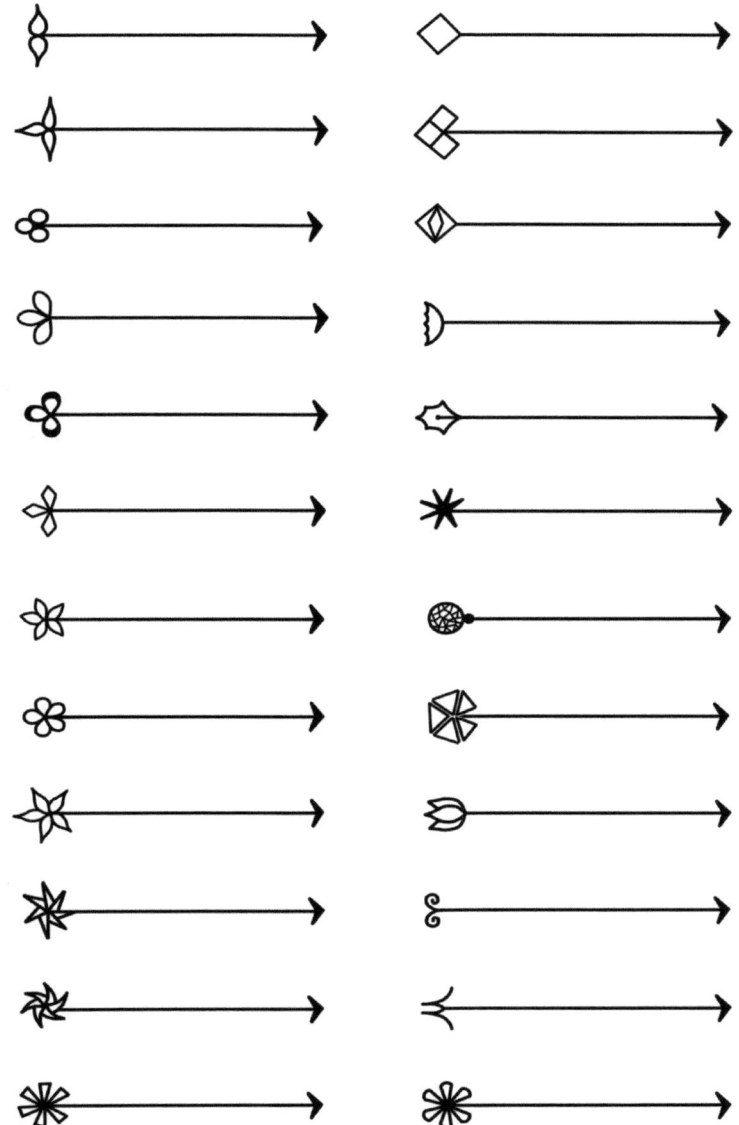

85

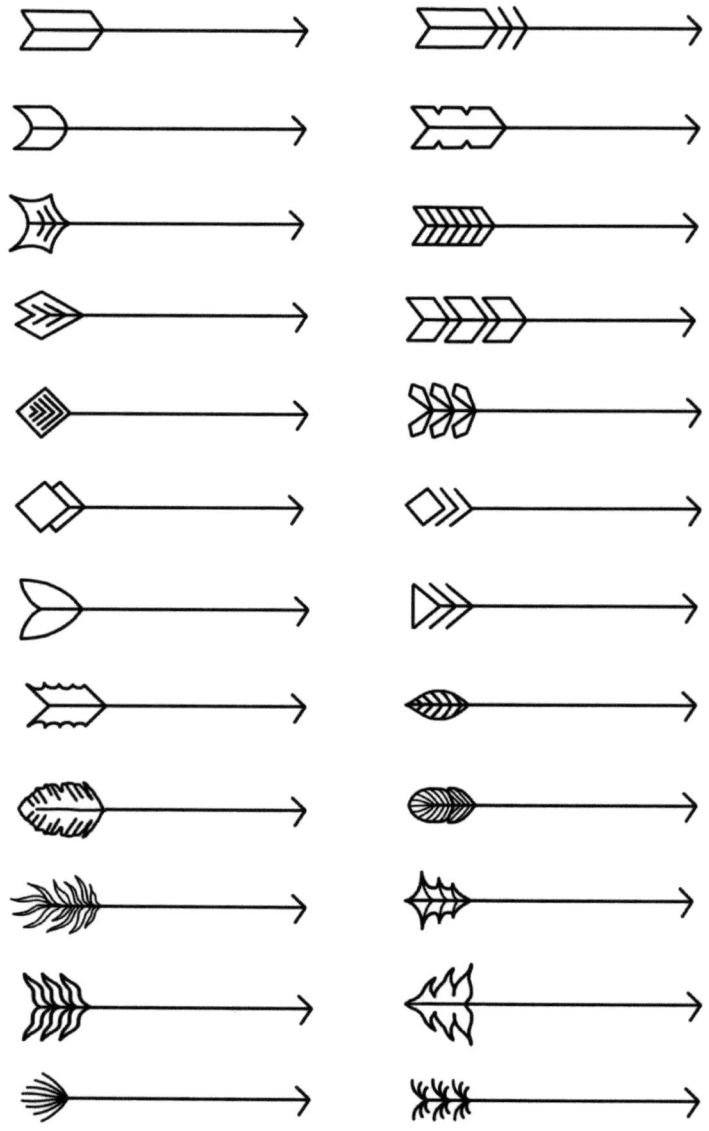

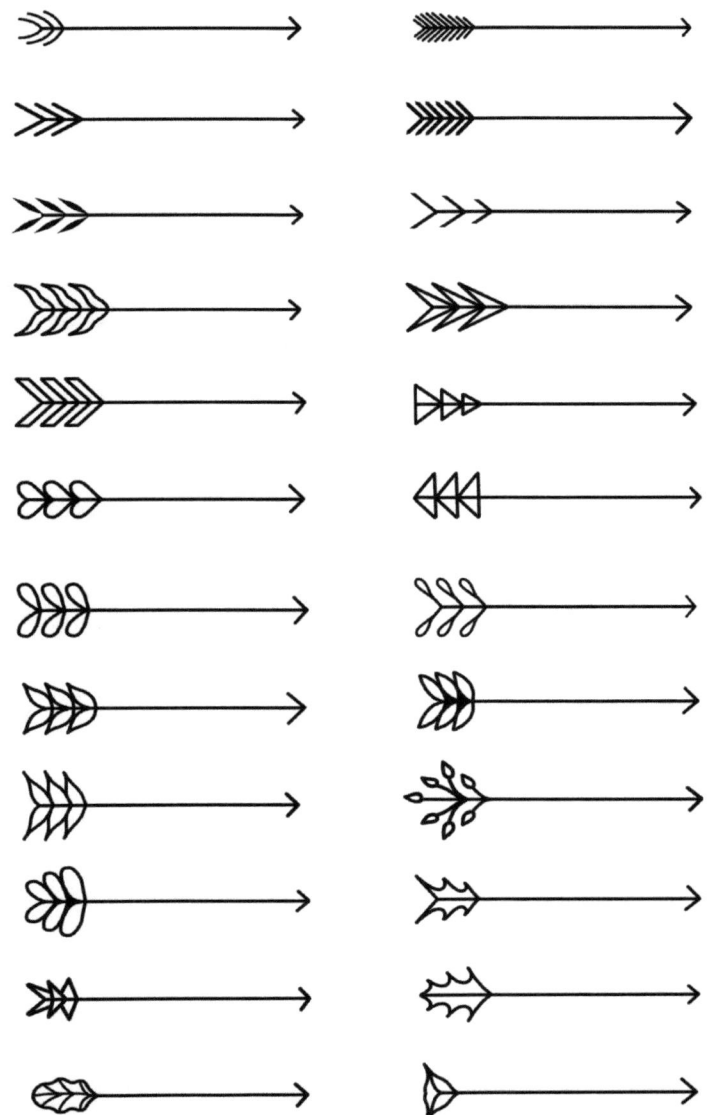

87

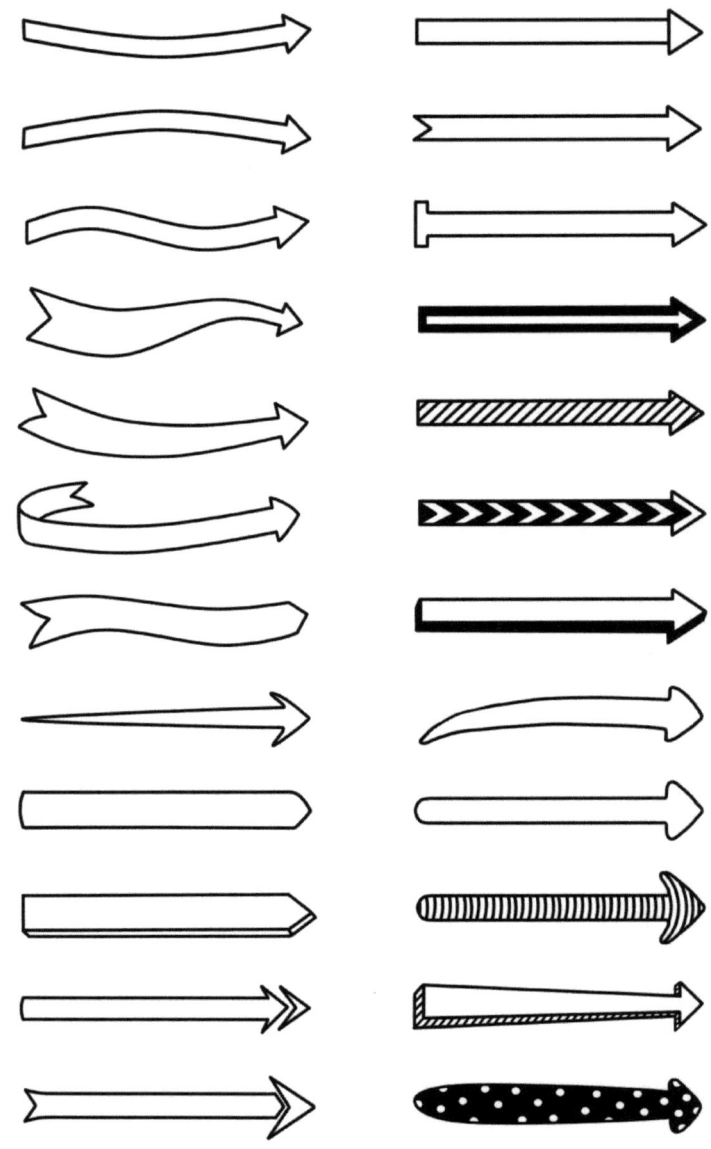

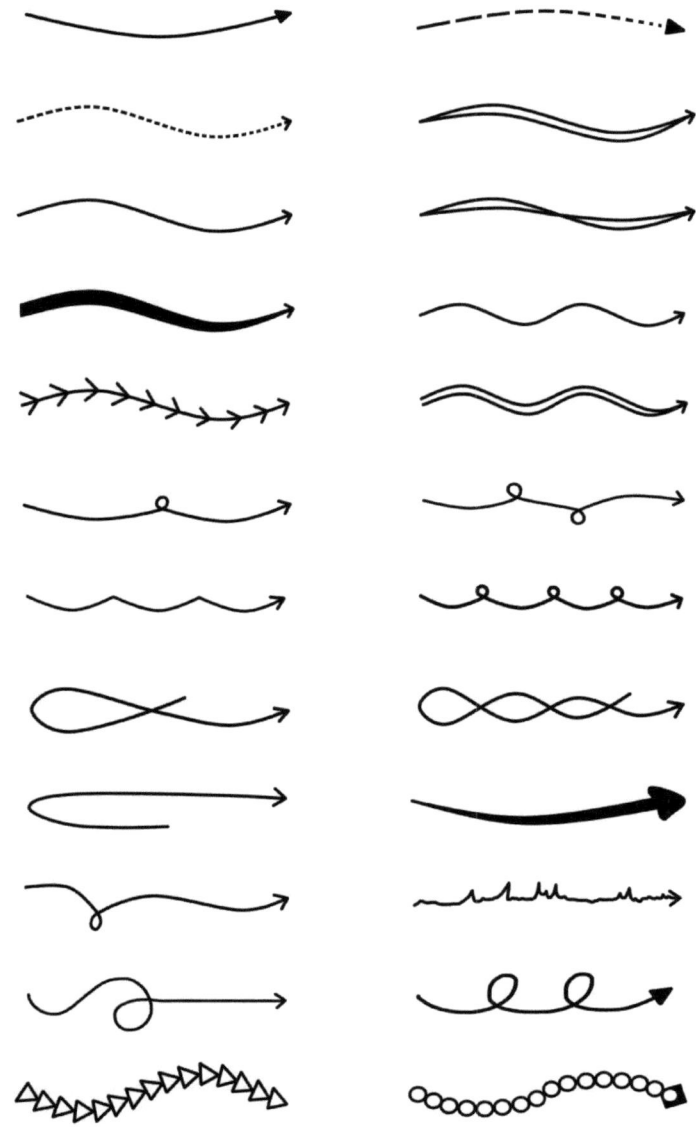

89

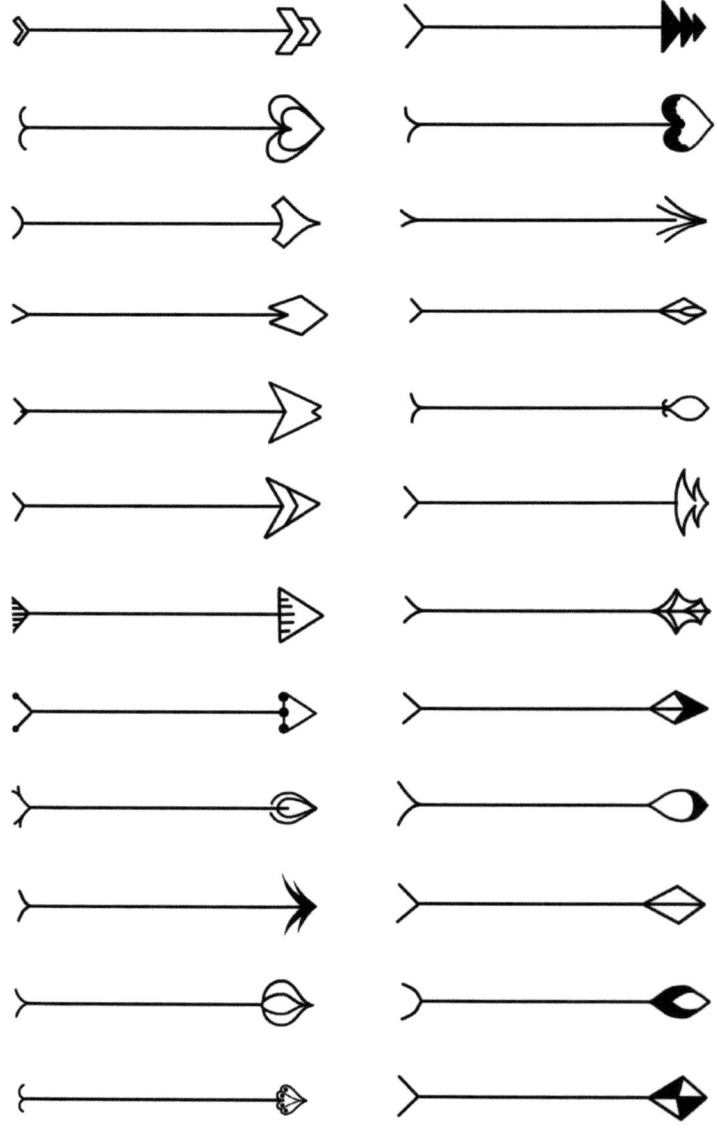

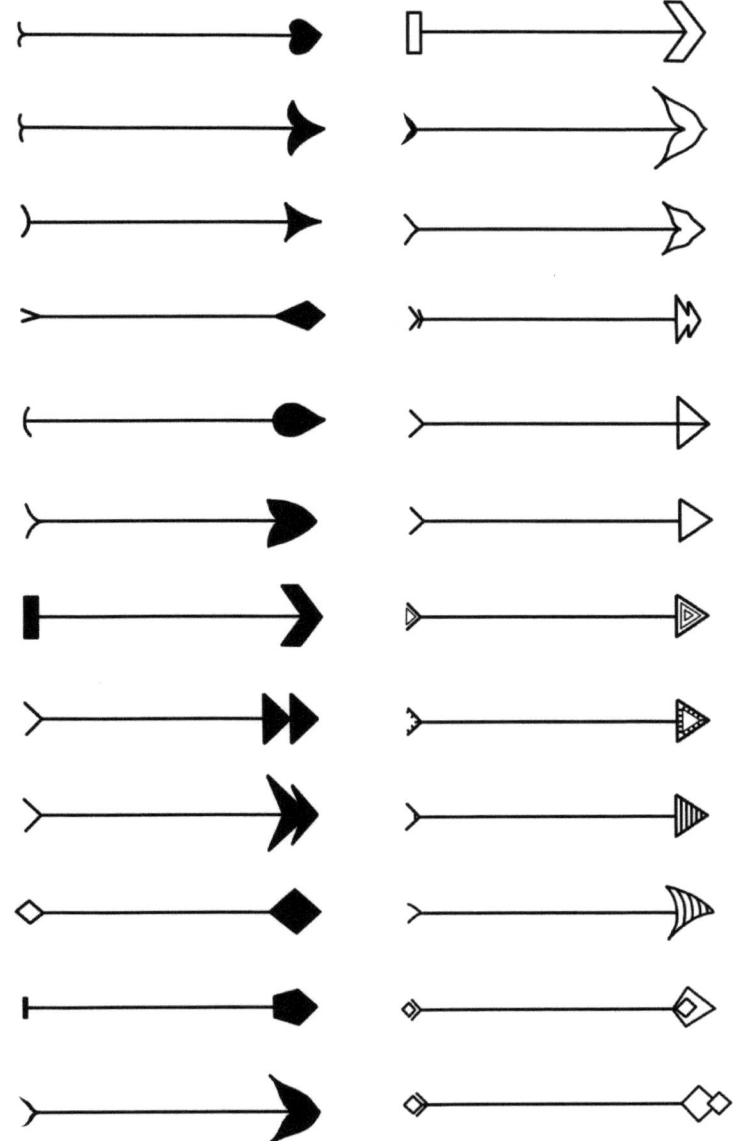

Last Christmas
Wham

My wish list:

Christkindlmarkt

dreams come true

Doodles

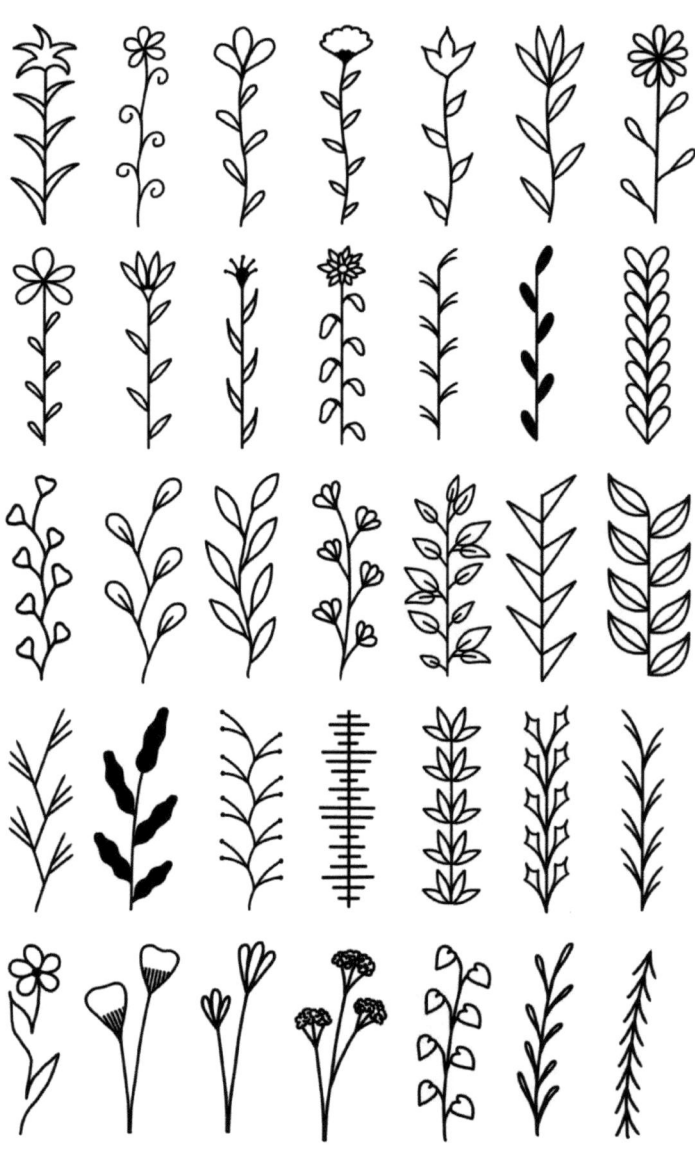